I0815769

Upgrade Your House

Rebuild, Renovate, and Reimagine Your Home

gestalten

Contents

Renovate, Don't Recreate

A home is more than a physical structure: it is a reflection of its owner's personality; a sanctuary and place of rest; a harbor for valuable objects and memories; and a place for people and families to grow. As a house's owners inevitably change, and their needs and desires along with them, it is only natural to assume that the house should change, too—whether that be as drastic of a transformation as tearing down walls and building new rooms, or as simple as buying additional furniture or new artifacts and belongings.

Lucky owners may accumulate more capital over the course of time and choose to invest it back into their homes. Especially at a time of housing market instability and general economic uncertainty, many owners choose to upgrade their existing assets rather than sell and buy new property, finding that renovations feel more personal, customizable, and accessible than buying new homes altogether. Others will seek out new properties as their buying power grows, but nevertheless opt to renovate to ensure the space best meets their needs. Taking a macro view, architects, designers, and policymakers around the world have been emphasizing and incentivizing adaptive reuse as an alternative to full-scale demolition and construction. The home-improvement industry has been growing steadily, spurred by motivated owners and incentives from the building industry (working with local governments). Globally, with the cost of living increasing and sustainability becoming a more central focus, many are turning to renovations as an available means of making their long-sought dream-house a physical reality.

This book is meant to serve as a resource for homeowners and designers either considering or already undertaking the renovation process. Here, we provide upgrade tips alongside examples of successful refurbishment projects from which readers can learn and gain inspiration. The compiled projects and articles should serve both as encouragement and as a ready pool of ideas for whatever size renovation is at hand, whether large or small; they prove that even an "ugly duckling" home can, with guidance, metamorphose into a beautiful swan.

The houses featured in this volume are the cream of the crop, having won awards and global coverage for their innovative renovations of existing buildings and homes. But these stunning spaces often began from manifestly humble roots. Representing a diverse array of styles, techniques, materials, climates, cultures, and clients, these fashionable, contemporary homes find themselves born from retrofitted Victorian cottages; dilapidated rural barns and cabins; abandoned industrial warehouses and factories. Many of the new furnishings sheath sleek modern aesthetics into the raw envelope of the existing structure; others mobilize the building's original style and implement a vintage or rustic design scheme. Wherever the reader may be in the world, they are sure to find inspiration from the array of cultural traditions represented in the following pages: Flemish bungalows follow Chinese courtyard houses, which are presented abreast of Spanish social housing projects. Designed for a global audience, the upcoming spreads—charting a swath of different design styles, refurbishment approaches, and preservation techniques—are bound to contain useful ideas and information for your journey.

The informational articles tackle key aspects of the renovation process, providing flexible recommendations and ideas around space arrangement, kitchen design, bathroom refurbishment, and more. Not sure where to start when it comes to implementing sustainable lighting for your home? Looking for options for kitchen-appliance upgrades? The tips compiled in this book are intended to cater to a wide audience—from new, untrained DIY renovators to licensed architects and interior designers. These guidelines keep everything from sustainability and cost to aesthetics in mind, allowing readers to pick out information that aligns with their priorities and needs.

Regardless of the kind of renovation you aim to undertake, *Upgrade Your House* serves as a trusted, informative companion, offering inspiration and practical advice to empower you through your home-makeover journey. From simple and affordable purchases and updates to larger-scale upgrades and dramatic refurbishments, the following tips equip you with the knowledge and confidence to make informed decisions and achieve your (or your client's) vision of the perfect home.

That said, we invite you to explore the ensuing pages with a few preliminary suggestions.

Always start by making a plan—and smoothing out the kinks and details of that plan to the greatest degree possible. Something unexpected is bound to happen, but putting a plan in place limits the number of extenuating issues that could arise. Then, begin with the dirty, invasive work: rearrange or expand your space, rip walls out, and cut new windows as needed. Always redo your kitchen and bathroom first, as they are vital areas of use; otherwise, you can spread your renovations out over months or even years, continuing as time and money allow. Only commence with decoration, refurnishing, and restyling after large-scale structural changes are fully complete, so as to avoid dust and dirt staining new walls and furniture.

With this rough schedule in mind, take a look at the collection of homes and articles assembled here. We hope the following ideas and inspirations will help you unlock the latent potential of your home, unleash your creativity, and elevate your space to new heights.

(Opposite) Feina Studio used an off-site prefabricated plywood system in the renovation of the Plywood House. The designers employed local artisans and materials when possible.

مسجد علي
MESKITA . ALI
20
Alarma

Four Stories of Raw and Historic Masonry

BSP 20 HOUSE
BY RAÚL SÁNCHEZ ARCHITECTS
BARCELONA, SPAIN
SQUAT → FAMILY HOME

A geometric-patterned metallic front door marks the entrance to BSP 20 House by Raúl Sánchez Architects, hinting at Barcelona's classic hydraulic mosaics that the client dearly loves. Once used as a squat, the dilapidated state of this home meant it was in severe need of repair. Damaged floors, weak stairs, and the need to update the structure in line with regulations meant that most of the interior was demolished. However, traces of its original construction—including the facades, arches, and scruffy raw brickwork—remain unaltered, indicating the building's somewhat messy history. A cylindrical spiral stairwell runs the entire height of the four-story home and is topped with a skylight, uniting the interior and displaying the surprising height of the slim property. White walls, microcement, hydraulic cement mosaic and oak floors, and lacquered wood ceilings abound, with touches of metal in the kitchen. Seven stainless-steel cylinders that visibly run the height of the edifice conduct the electrical system, plumbing, and more.

(This page) The client wished for the original hydraulic cement mosaics to be retained and restored. (Opposite) The slim exterior frame hints at the home's modest 215 square feet (20 m²) per floor.

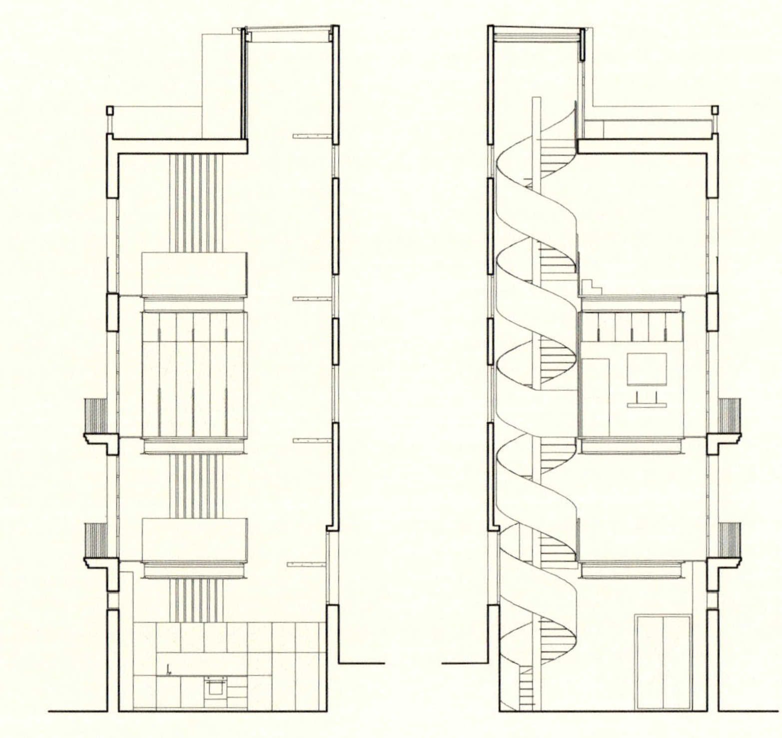

(Opposite) The architects purposely left pockmarked brickwork raw and unsealed. A glass floor panel beside the balcony doors allows vertical views through the building.

GORDON STRONG AUTOMOBILE OBJECTIVE . FRANK LLOYD WRIGHT
Sigurd Lewerentz
carloscarpa

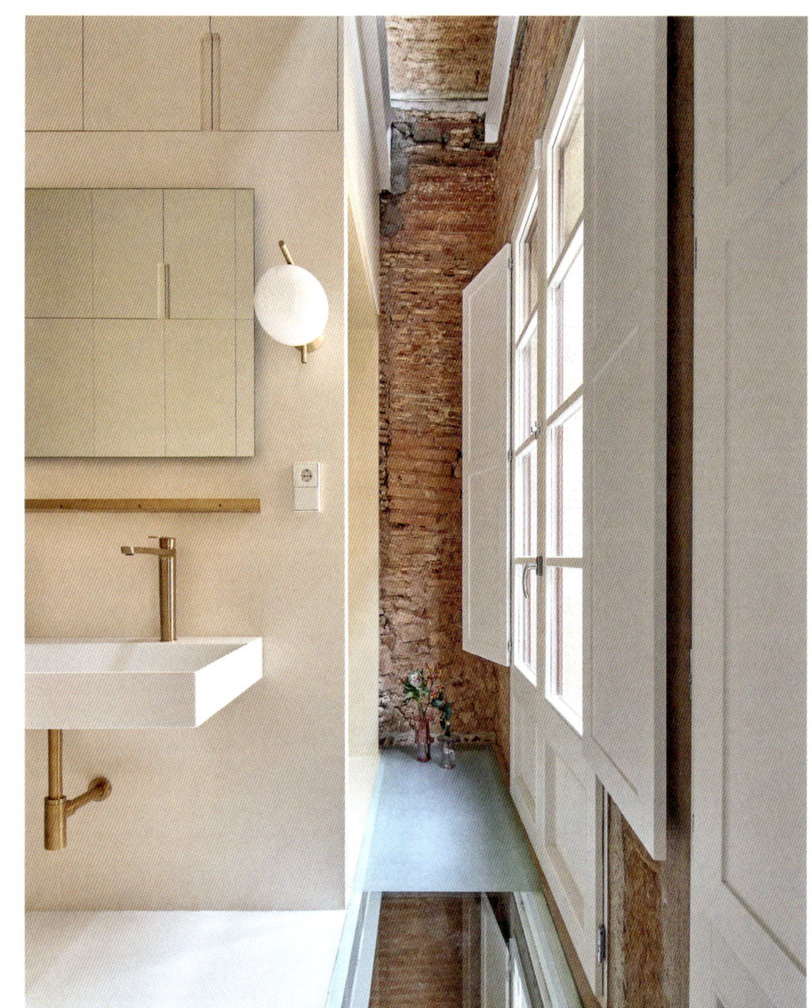

(Right) A timber-clad rooftop terrace reveals views across historic apartments in Barcelona's El Born district. (Above, right) The bathroom is paneled with lacquered wood and brass details.

When Two Become One: An Adaptive Apartment

MG08 BY BURR STUDIO
MADRID, SPAIN
COMMERCIAL SPACES → FLEXIBLE DWELLING

Burr Studio designed MG08 to change alongside the lives of its owners. The architects split the apartment into two separate dwellings divided by an acoustic protection wall—allowing its young owners to rent out one side until they became more financially stable. The wall can then be moved to increase or decrease space on either side of the building as the owners' needs shift and change. Over the years, the ground-floor space of the Madrid building housed a variety of industrial, commercial, and sporting ventures. With the selection of material, the architects referenced the building's history, from the sunshine-yellow tiled wall in the shared areas, which elicits locker-room aesthetics, to the raw treatment of cinder block walls, plywood, and concrete floors hinting at an industrial past. The kitchen was developed with Cubro, a design studio specializing in adapting Ikea shelving to fit the user's needs. Here, it provides significant storage space not just for the kitchen, but for the whole apartment.

(Opposite) Vibrant yellow tiles brighten the kitchen and living area, separating these spaces from the bedroom and bathroom. (Above) The kitchen faces the courtyard with a view through large glass sliding doors.

TALKING
HEADS
MOR
ENAS
BIZNAGA
JUVENTUD
JUCHÉ
MONSTRUOS
PUNK 365
ATLAS OF BRUTAL
ARCHITECTURE

(Left) A colorful array of books, art, and plants line the timber shelving, behind which stands an industrial wall made of cinder blocks. Nearby sits a white tulip-style table and chairs.

C'ERA UNA VOLTA IL WEST
C'ERA UNA VOLTA IL WEST
HENRY FONDA CLAUDIA CARDINALE JASON ROBARDS
CHARLES BRONSON PAOLO STOPPA

The interior materiality refers to typical elements of Spanish ground-floor spaces through its use of tiles, raw cement materials, and anti-fly curtains.

A Green Thumb's Home and Inner-City Garden

HOUSE TP BY DMVA ARCHITECTS
MECHELEN, BELGIUM
DERELICT RESIDENCE → PRIVATE HOME AND URBAN GARDEN

House TP is a small white home beside a church in Mechelen, a picturesque town between Brussels and Antwerp. A woman with a passion for gardening purchased the ruined house with the wish of cultivating a space for urban farming. To compensate for the shaded courtyard that receives little sun, the architects removed a back section of the building, leaving just one steel beam. Additional beams were added and painted yellow, and upon this a greenhouse was placed. The floating garden is now a statement part of the residence. The facade was whitewashed to lighten the building (while also allowing the historic scars on the frontage to remain), and the garage was opened to the street, with steel blinds to provide privacy while illuminating the once-dark part of the street. The bedroom was placed downstairs and the living room and terrace upstairs in order to welcome more sunshine into the living spaces. Minimal interiors were wrapped in oriented strand board—a cost-effective and visually warm material.

(Opposite and left) The whitewashed exterior of House TP stands out against the abutting vernacular brickwork. A passage opens under the home, leading from the garage at the front to the backyard.

(Left and right) Bright-yellow structural beams suspend a green-house above the dark courtyard, ensuring that it receives enough sun despite the high walls of the neighboring church.

A Colorful Extension to a Victorian Cottage

IL NIDO HOUSE BY ANGELUCCI ARCHITECTS
MELBOURNE, AUSTRALIA
WORKERS' COTTAGE → FAMILY HOME

A renovated Victorian-era workers' cottage, Il Nido House, was designed by Angelucci Architects and references the owner's family migration from Italy to Australia. The 19th-century workers' abode is perched on a corner in the north part of the city of Melbourne, within the suburb to which the client's grandparents first moved. The original brickwork facade was extended along the block and to a second story, and it features a Welsh-slate, scale-like accent mimicking the color of the original roof. The scale motif is continued in handmade blue and aquamarine tiles in the private central courtyard, which can be opened to merge the inside living spaces with the outside world. Curves soften the interior, with an oval, marble-topped table in the kitchen-dining room, elongated oval touchpoint handles on the kitchen cabinetry, a serpentine built-in timber wall in the living area, and arched doorways. Color is meticulously used to define each area, with the kitchen featuring fresh pops of green and the living room warmed with maroon, orange, and pink hues.

(Opposite) Updated features, such as the arching doorway and an abstract Welsh-slate scale pattern, define the modern extension, while continuing brickwork links the old to the new.

(Above, right) The living room brims with eclectic shapes, from the sharp stairs and the Gerrit Rietveld–style armchair to the curves of the carpet, side table, and timber-battened wall.

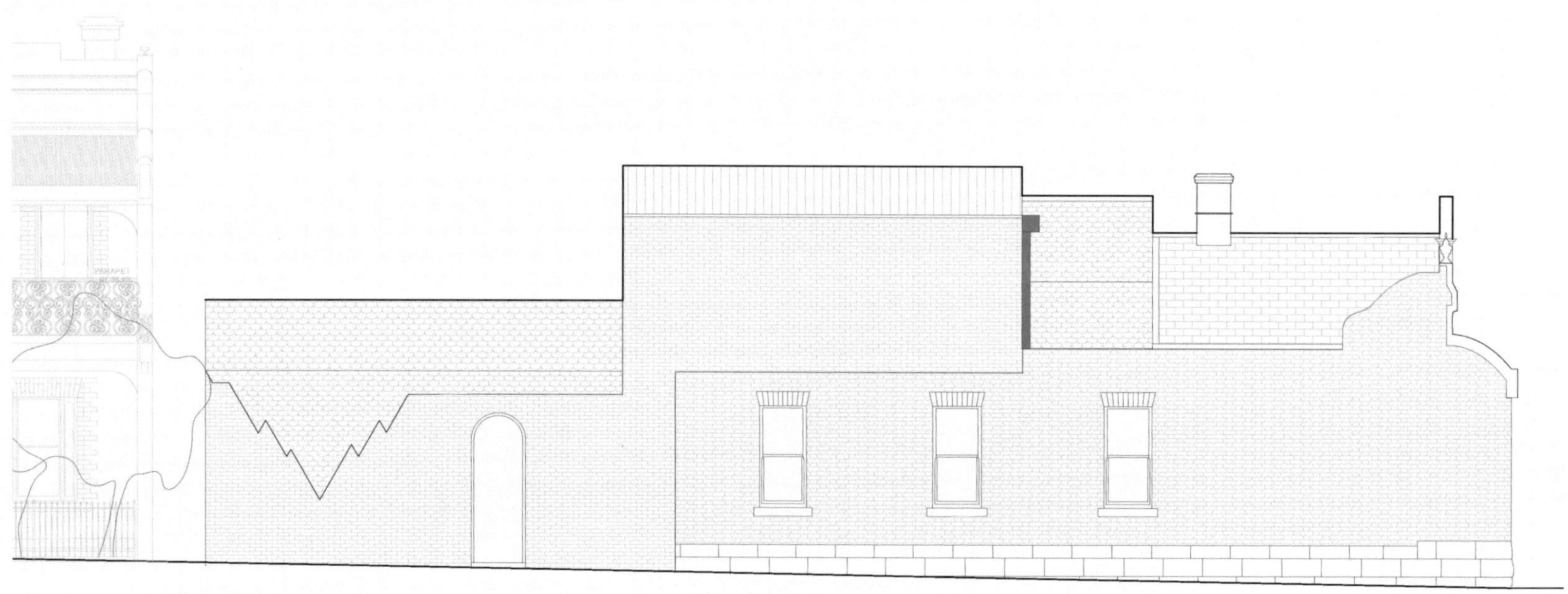

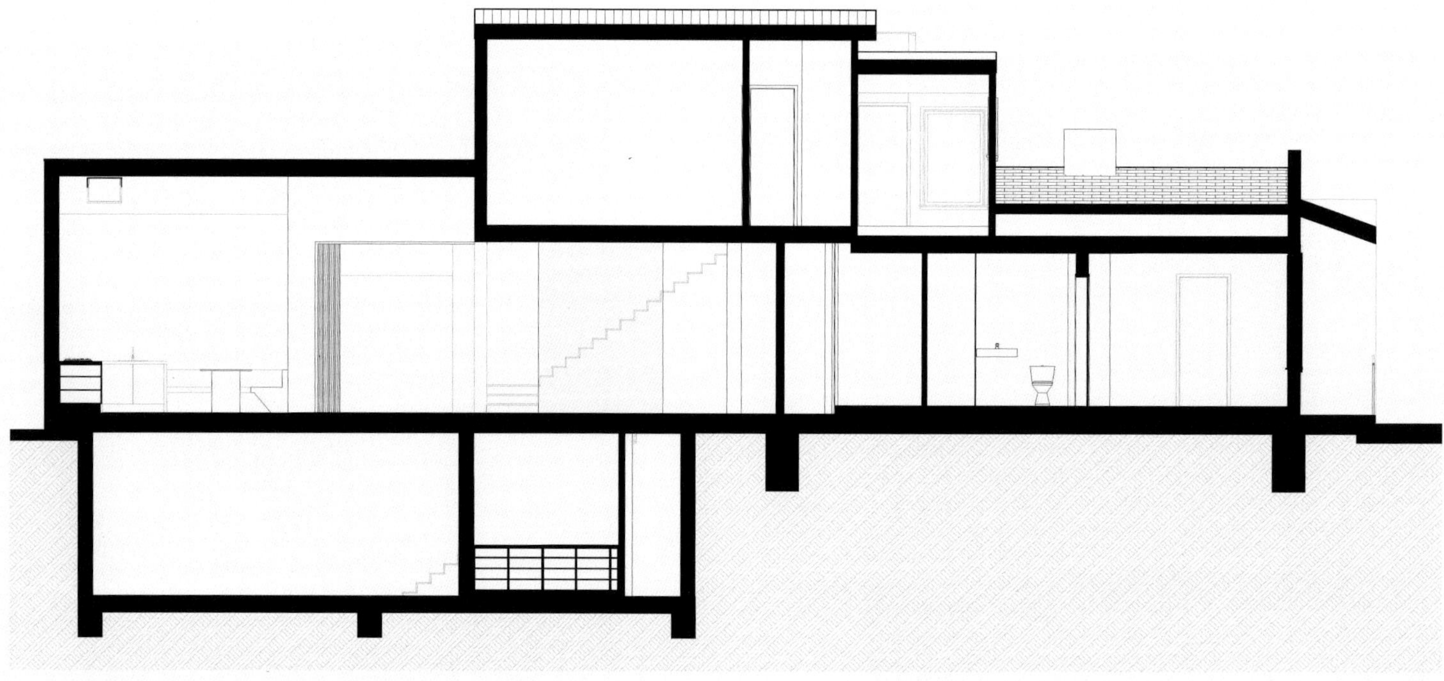

The architects transformed the floor plan into a family home for a couple and their four small children. The house now has two living rooms, three bedrooms, and three bathrooms.

(Right) A skylight in the slim bathroom allows light into the private space. The compact design compensates for the home's relatively small size on a 1,160-square foot (108 m²) block of land.

The Refurbishment of a Compact London Terrace

LITTLE BROWNINGS BY ARCHMONGERS ARCHITECTS
LONDON, U.K.
MIDCENTURY TERRACE → MODERN HOME

Down a pathway framed by blue and red bricks, a yellow door beneath terra-cotta brindles leads into Little Brownings. Archmongers Architects renovated the 1960s Forest Hill terrace to modernize it and added an extension in place of the previous lean-to. "The skeleton of this midcentury house was good, but the kitchen and hallway circulation needed to be redesigned to better integrate the main living spaces," says Margaret Bursa, Managing Partner of Archmongers. As such, the front addition hosts a compact kitchen and utility room with exposed Douglas fir beams and an "up-and-over" window that visually expands the space. The kitchen also spotlights Carrara marble benches and a bespoke pink semi-circular concrete counter with gray speckled tiling underfoot. The tiling delineates the kitchen and dining area from the timber-floored living room. From the living room, floor-to-ceiling windows open the space to a leafy garden, while stairs lead to the renovated upper level of the terrace house in southeast London.

Large windows and a clever use of space make the most of the home's small floor plan. Archmongers Architects' design extended and updated the home while retaining its midcentury style.

(Opposite) A nod to the home's midcentury history, Marcel Breuer's steel-frame Cesca Chairs—which rose to popularity in the 1960s—line the dining table.

Rescued from Abandonment

LOFT STUDY HOUSE #1 BY ACHA ZABALLA ARCHITECTS
BILBAO, SPAIN
COMMERCIAL SPACES → SOCIAL HOUSING

Acha Zaballa Architects transforms boarded-up shop fronts into much-needed social housing. At the base of a gray building in Bilbao is a surprising pop of orange belonging to Loft Study House #1, a pilot in Acha Zaballa's public housing project for the Department of Territorial Planning, Housing, and Transport of the local Basque government. The accordion window bars—once protecting a wide glass shop facade—now act as a layer of marigold-hued privacy for new inhabitants. Inside, while universal design and essential domestic elements are integral to the apartment's success, the architects transcend basic expectations by ensuring it is cozy, modern, and beautiful. Herringbone floors and curved corners soften the space, while forest-green tiling, mint accents, and orange cabinetry create a unique identity for the residence, rejecting cookie-cutter social housing style. An exercise in adaptive reuse, Loft Study House #1 revitalizes streets, provides housing, and sustainably repurposes existing buildings, ultimately solving a multifaceted problem.

(This page) Frosted glass allows light into the ground-floor apartment while also providing ample privacy. (Opposite) Bright orange security bars add color to the gray block.

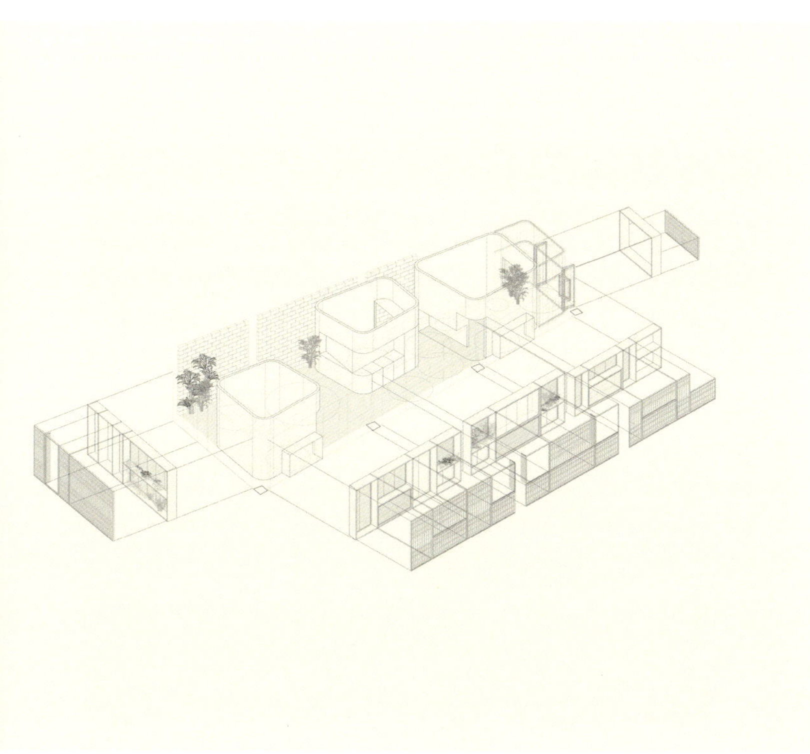

Two-toned green tiles and contrasting bright orange cabinetry were purposely chosen to create a warm aesthetic and overcome the often sluggish energy of the ground floor.

97

A Compact Spanish Row House Receives a Refresh

105JON BY VALLRIBERA ARQUITECTES
VALLÈS OCCIDENTAL, SPAIN
OLD ROW HOUSE → FAMILY HOME

Bold pops of blue, a motif that continues throughout the home, enlivens the lime-mortar facade of this Spanish row house. Throughout 105JON, elements of the initial home are paired with juxtaposing modern counterparts; exposed brick walls in their original patchwork form contrast with clean plaster walls and engineered timber. Overhead, sections of the roof feature original exposed timber beams, with some bowing due to the weight of time. New overhead beams stand out in blue, at once mimicking their original exposed-beam counterparts and serving as a contrast with their vibrant azure hue. The architects purposely maintained the footprint of the home, yet aimed to capitalize on space and improve thermal performance. The roof, facades, and new floor are all insulated, and skylights were added to increase natural light. The height of the historic building was also taken advantage of, with the addition of a mezzanine to allow space for children's rooms, a bathroom, and a study.

Azure-blue accents run throughout the row house, from the front door and window bars to the new overhead beams, upstairs balustrade, and vinyl flooring in the children's rooms.

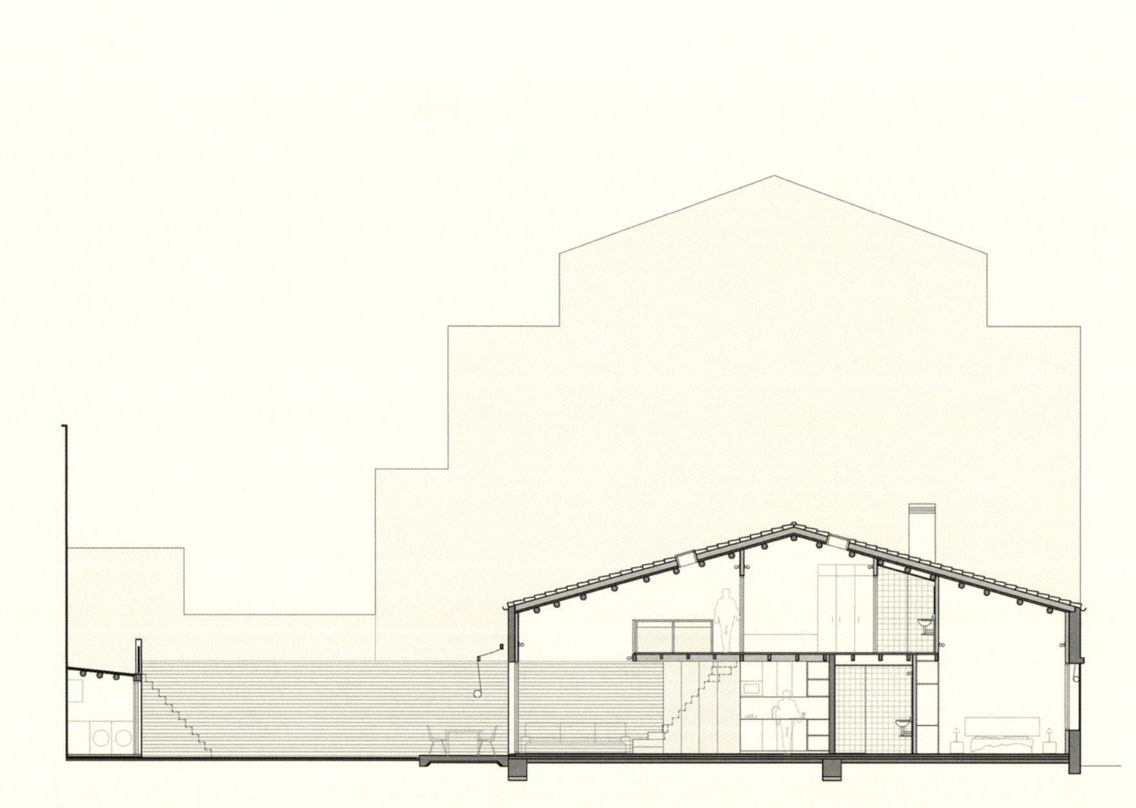

The basic structure of the home was not altered, but the owners capitalized on the lofty ceilings to add a mezzanine level for the children's rooms, a bathroom, and a study.

Moving House

How to Find the Right Place

Moving isn't an easy process: researching, uprooting, and transporting your belongings takes a great deal of energy, consideration, and logistics. Putting in the work to make sure your new place is the *right* place—in other words, selecting from your options with sufficient care and consideration—is one of the most important parts of this process.

Vetting the location of your new house should be the first step. Are you looking for a big city? A small town? Something in between? Does the cost of living match your budget, and do you have job prospects, childcare options, or nearby grocery stores as needed? There are plenty of factors that must go into selecting a new destination. Yet arguably just as important—if not more so—is the process of finding a new home.

Choosing Your Home

Ideally, you might want to move into a house that already perfectly suits your needs; however, not only are these rare to find, but they are usually more expensive and almost always come with concessions to the homeowner's envisioned lifestyle. Moving into a home with the expectation of renovating or upgrading can be comparatively inexpensive and generally more practical if you have specific requirements in mind, especially if the remodeling occurs at a smaller scale. From minor adjustments like painting cabinets to major endeavors such as building a new wing, renovations come in many shapes and sizes—but, if executed with attentiveness and care, they almost always make a big difference.

How, then, can a new homeowner choose the right place with such upgrades in mind? First, the home itself must accord with your means: perhaps most importantly, what can you afford? New homeowners have to be realistic about budget constraints and allocating funds. A stately manor in the countryside may seem alluring at first glance, but if money is a constraint or major renovations are expected, a homey cabin in the woods may ultimately prove to be a better investment. A related consideration is style: are you looking for something traditional? Modern? Timeless? Traditional homes can exude an aura of comfort or refinement and reveal their owner's attentiveness to history or convention. Alternatively, modern homes may feel younger and more chic. For homeowners with the appropriate budget and sufficient interest, combinations of classical and contemporary architecture are well-lauded in design circles around the world, with some of today's most famous homes emerging from a well-designed modern rehabilitation of older orthodox designs. At the end of the day, however, the homeowner's style preferences come first.

Planning for Structural Renovation

Once these general constraints have narrowed down the pool of possibilities, homeowners should consider their budget for renovations alongside their specific requisites for the space. How many bedrooms and bathrooms do you or your family require? What size do you want these rooms to be? How large or small can your kitchen be, and what kind of appliances would you like? If you have your eye on a home that fails to meet these basic needs, do you have the budget, time, and resources to adapt the space before you move in? And, importantly, does the existing space lend itself to the renovations you intend on to make?

New homeowners who plan for large-scale renovations—such as new wings or rooms—should always consider first whether the renovations are possible given the existing materials and state of the home; and second, how the additions will complement the existing structure to ensure the full layout stays cohesive or organized. Some homes lend themselves to such changes more than others. Older buildings, for example, may contain harmful substances that are easily released during the renovation process—especially asbestos. Such toxins require professional removal and can delay a renovation or inflate the cost if not accounted for. Brick buildings are often more difficult

to renovate than wooden ones, as new wings will either have to match the original brick and mortar or cleverly circumvent the issue with innovative design. The same issue tends to arise with beautiful historic homes that retain handmade detailing or era-specific materials; while wiring, plumbing, and window treatments lean toward the pricier side for structures made of older materials. In some areas, state regulations dictate the extent to which a historic home can be renovated, sometimes requiring the preservation or imitation of existing materials. Often, homeowners will accept this sacrifice as an unfortunate consequence of stylistic preference, and the initial high cost may even pay off over time. Nevertheless, materials are an essential consideration when buying a new home, especially when renovations are expected.

Homes with unusual layouts may also be more difficult to design additions around, and preservation may come at the cost of convenience or livability. Some older homes have strange configurations, including odd passageways, tiny rooms, steep staircases, and the occasional chute. Such quirks may prove to be easily amended or even useful over the course of a renovation, but they always require additional thought. Even some common layouts may prove difficult to design around, especially if you have specific needs. If your family values privacy, for example, a shotgun house—however cheap, convenient, or desirably located—may not be the right choice unless you are ready to make significant changes to the original plan. Even if you envision a multiroom addition, the existing layout should play a major part in your decision.

Delegating Space

Smaller-scale upgrades immensely benefit from close attention to the initial structure as well. New room additions can be made by making the most of the original building without expanding its footprint. New home buyers without the need for a car might consider buying a house with a garage, only to convert the garage into an additional room and bathroom. Those with fewer items could convert an attic or basement used for storage into supplementary rooms. A particularly space-conscious buyer might find themselves drawn to a house with a staircase closet, hoping to convert it into a half bathroom, a pantry, a bookshelf, or a reading nook. Approaching the buying process with a keen eye for potential upgrades, while keying in to the oddities of the existing space, opens a world of possibilities for improved, owner-specific living.

System Updates

Naturally, buyers must be attentive to less romantic concerns, too. If you plan on making upgrades to the home's electricity system, heating and cooling, or plumbing—or if you intend to add new rooms, requiring a change to any of these systems—make sure that the existing arrangement won't cause unnecessary difficulties. For example, if you build new rooms, can your existing heating and cooling equipment handle the new square footage? If not, how difficult or costly would it be to install a new system or upgrade the existing one? Is it as easy as adding or replacing an external unit, or will you have to open walls and add soffits to install new ducts altogether? You may not think these details would be enough to dissuade you from buying a particular home, but they should be factored into your budget and schedule. Each of these components should play into the larger picture as you make choices to find your next place, however small they may initially seem.

Finding the right place is a difficult process, especially when you have renovations to consider. But when it's all said and done, assessing each of these variables, however minute, will be incredibly rewarding. Searching for a new home is a significant undertaking, and it absolutely must be treated as such—with care, thoughtfulness, and consideration.

(Above) This Victorian-era worker's cottage is now a tasteful inner-city Melbourne house (see p. 22). (Opposite) Hourré was transformed from a Basque farmhouse ruin into a family home (see p. 238).

The Metamorphosis of a 16th-Century Ruin

LA FAGE BY PLAN COMÚN
SAINT-BEAUZILE, FRANCE
DILAPIDATED HOUSE → COUNTRYSIDE HOME

Set in a glade within forested hills north of the Pyrenees, this updated early modern period home spotlights beautiful stone masonry and raw, natural surfaces. Plan Común updated the home, which previously lay in a state of partial ruin. Constrained by budgetary limitations, the architects focused on minimal changes to radically transform the house. The ground-floor barn became a central living room. On the floor directly above, the removal of a section of the roof created an open-air bathroom with spectacular views. Repurposed materials and savvy additions allowed the designers to do more with less: a partially collapsed barn wall became a cyclopean wall, and the lime hemp on the facade acts as bio-sourced insulation. Prefabricated beams, slabs, concrete blocks, and cyclopean concrete poured on-site enhance—rather than compete with—the existing raw masonry materials. A natural swimming pool with biological filtration sits in a field of grass beside the home. To reduce energy costs, a minimal part of the house can be heated during the winter.

Eight identical openings across the renovated sections of the home allow increased ventilation and natural light, and make the most of the wide, unimpeded views.

Natural Materials Combine in a Rural Warehouse

CHOLAN NESTS HOUSE BY MARIE COMBETTE AND DANIEL MORENO FLORES/LA CABINA DE LA CURIOSIDAD
PERUCHO, ECUADOR
BLOCK-WALL WAREHOUSE → RURAL RESIDENCE

Cholan Nests House sits in a rural area 22 miles (35 km) outside the Ecuadorian capital of Quito. Once a warehouse, the structure received a slew of patches over the years. Finally, the property's owners opted for a complete restoration to realize its full potential. The building required a range of improvements to fix ongoing issues, from minimal light and a lack of connection with the surrounding landscape to dampness in the walls and a decaying heavy clay roof. The architects suggested a new metal roof with an affordable, lightweight interior structure made of natural materials, including *eucalyptus pingo* and chopped cane, coconut fiber for insulation, and egg cartons as acoustic softeners. The new roof rises above the original ceiling, allowing light through new windows between the roof and the original walls. The heightened ceiling allows for two new bedrooms to be suspended above the main living area. Additionally, unique features from the earlier home were salvegeable, such as a large porthole-like window and original block walls.

The new windows above the original walls allow increased light, ventilation, and views. It is now possible to see nearby fields, distant mountains, and a nearby Cholan tree through them.

The floating forms hold two new bedrooms and two new “nests” for working and art. The unique construction is handcrafted, thereby satisfying the owners’ aesthetic sensibilities.

Honoring a 20th-Century Industrial Building

18TH STREET LOFT BY SÍOL STUDIOS
SAN FRANCISCO, CA, USA
CANDY FACTORY → INDUSTRIAL LOFT

Large black iron-framed windows that are characteristic of early 20th-century San Franciscan warehouses sweep across one wall of the 18th Street Loft. The apartment—previously a candy factory for the American producer See's Candies before being converted into a basic loft—was renovated to modernize it while enhancing the original aesthetic of the building. "We really wanted to honor the history of the building, not conceal it," says Síol Studios architect Jessica Weigley. To execute this goal, original materials, such as raw concrete, were revealed and furniture was locally sourced. A smooth and slightly reflective concrete floor acts as a counterweight to the high board-formed concrete ceiling and raw columns. Small touches demarcate different zones of the living area; off-white kitchen cabinetry and neutral hexagonal tiles softly contrast with the floors; while a feature wall of rich, dark blue indicates the dining area. The space is both welcoming and homely, yet still references its manufacturing history.

Animal-skin rugs, plush leather, soft furnishings, and plants soften this former industrial space. Parts of the building's historic style remain untouched, such as the raw ceiling and pylons.

VIKING
TARTINE BREAD
TOKYO
FLOUR + WATER
EAT GOOD FOOD
TARTINE ALL DAY
JERUSALEM

Bicycle racks become art on one wall of the apartment. Hanging one above the other, the two-bike storage system saves space and creates a unique visual element.

A Car Factory Receives a Domestic Revamp

MICHIGAN LOFT BY VLADIMIR RADUTNY ARCHITECTS
CHICAGO, IL, USA
AUTOMOBILE WAREHOUSE → MEZZANINE APARTMENT

Exposed brick walls; blonde timber cladding; and black, gray, and charcoal accents merge under the cavernous concrete ceiling of this century-old structure. Once an automotive assembly warehouse and showroom, the early 20th-century Chicago structure underwent a prior conversion into a domestic residence, but its layout functioned poorly. To rectify this, Vladimir Radutny Architects refined and updated the interior. At the entrance, a cocooning timber-clad transition zone provides a warm welcome and removes the starkness from the warehouse aesthetic. In the living area, the home opens to lofty, double-height ceilings featuring theatrical suspended lighting. The "sleeping cube" is clad in black steel and lined internally with wood paneling, and is situated further from the exterior walls for greater noise and temperature control. The architects' restraint in tonal and material palette—paired with a selection of quality furniture and materials—has encapsulated the spirit of an ideal industrial conversion.

(Above) The entrance provides a warm, timber-clad welcome. (Left) Hanging pendant lights and a black-painted structural column accentuate the lofty height of the ceiling.

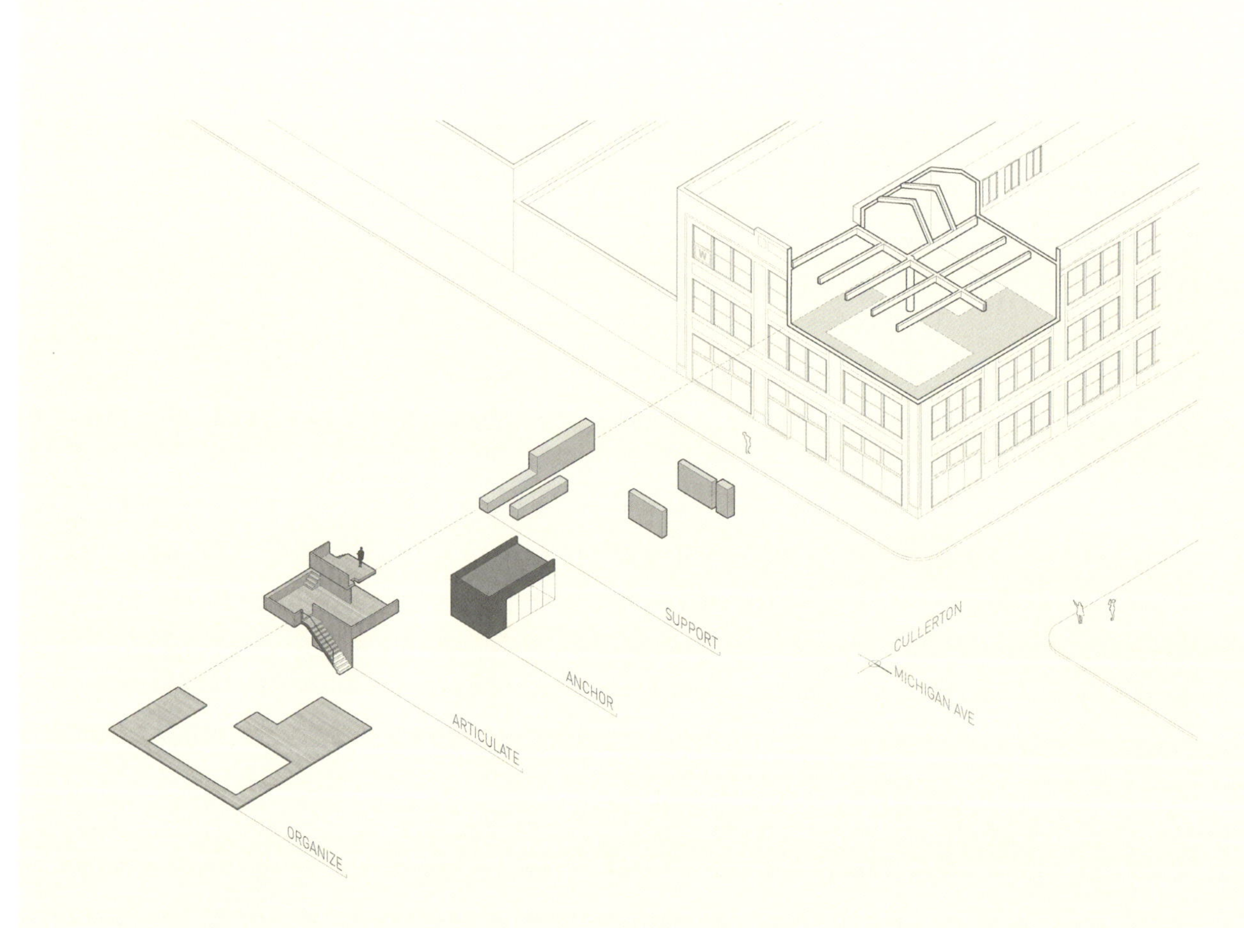

Timber and steel volumes were slotted into the concrete structure to compartmentalize the space. The steel section acts as a bedroom, while the timber provides a mezzanine.

Embracing Brutalism in a High-Rise Apartment

RST 13/14 BY STUDIO OKAMI
ANTWERP, BELGIUM
OFFICE SPACE → RESIDENTIAL APARTMENT

Owned by a couple who moved to the quiet, up-and-coming area on Antwerp's left bank, RST 13/14 was previously an office space. The brutalist complex was originally constructed by Belgian architect, urban planner, and designer Léon Stynen, who is recognized as a significant contributor to Antwerp's architectural landscape. An appreciation of the labor-intensive formwork is evident with its brutalist style. Colorful elements were added to soften the space, such as a powder-blue staircase and walkway, subtle peach floors, and playful artworks, furniture, and plants. Much of the furniture is true to the era of the building's original construction in the mid-20th century, with a patchwork De Sede DS88 sofa and Crate Chairs by Gerrit Rietveld. The kitchen island becomes a sculpture when not in use, but when utilized it is a high-functioning chef-level apparatus and staging area for the appliances stored in the Donald Judd-inspired wall unit.

(Opposite) The high-rise building is an iconic structure in Antwerp's Linkeroever, or Left Bank. (Above) Double-height windows expose the living room to copious light and views over the surroundings.

Large, colorful artworks from the owner's extensive collection feature on most walls of the apartment. The owner has a second duplex on the same floor for her art gallery and a B&B.

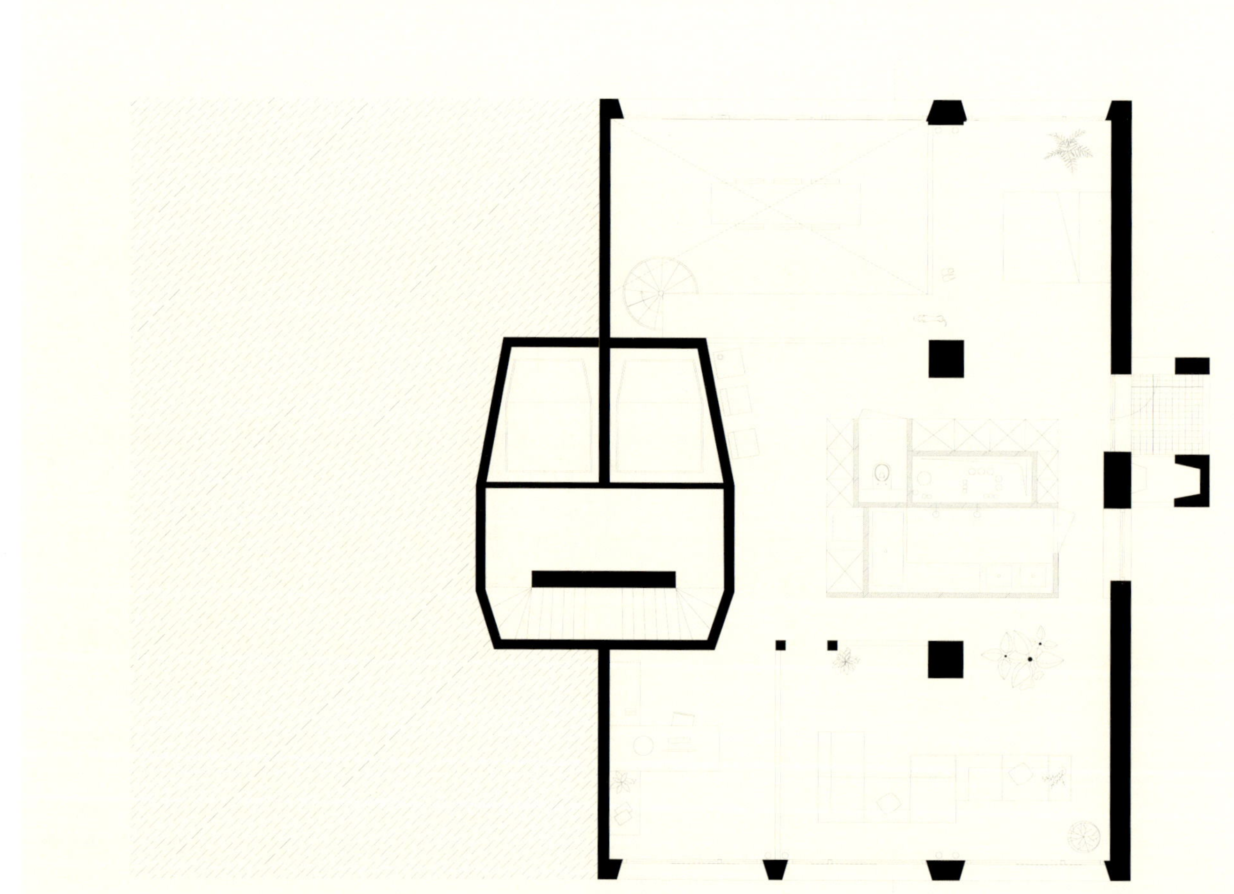

Previously a five-bedroom apartment, Studio Okami tore down the walls to reveal the textured concrete beneath and create an open-plan, single-bedroom loft.

The Breezy Charm of a Greek Subterranean Home

ILIOUPOLI APARTMENT
BY POINT SUPREME ARCHITECTS
ATHENS, GREECE
UNUSED BASEMENT → ONE-BEDROOM APARTMENT

Nestled in Athens's southeast neighborhood of Ilioupoli, this basement home is richly layered with vibrant tones, unconventional design details, and natural textures. Point Supreme Architects saw the potential of the formerly underutilized space, which is set partially below ground. Although the apartment presented the challenge of less light than upper levels, its subterranean nature and breeze-capturing abilities means it is cool, even in summer—a desirable asset in the Mediterranean. To allow sunlight to permeate throughout, the architects avoided opaque walls. Instead, timber partitions separate spaces, and a curtain between the bedroom and the living space allows adjustable privacy. A framed glass wall and a blue-and-white line of accented tiling also demarcates the bedroom. The apartment doesn't shy away from color: the pale blue bathroom echoes the blue tiling in the living space, while warm terracotta floors, crimson cabinetry, and accents of navy blue and orange warm the raw concrete columns and ceiling.

Point Supreme Architects gave a warm, unique character to this apartment, making the most of the 600-square-foot (56-m^2) partially subterranean space.

Floor types delineate each section of the house: white tiles mark the entry, terracotta tiles mark the living areas, blue marks the bathroom, and a line of blue and white creates a minimal divide for the bedroom.

The Conversion of an Abandoned City Brewery

BREWERY CONVERSION BY AUX
GHENT, BELGIUM
STEAM BREWERY → RESIDENCE

Located in Ghent, Belgium, this former brewery sits in an area historically known for its mix of housing, crafts, and smaller industries. It was damaged during World War I and abandoned after successive decades of stone masonry use. Years of neglect left it in a state of disrepair. The inside was empty, and parts of the brickwork had deteriorated. Architecture firm Aux restored the facade to its former state through a patchwork of old and new masonry. The interior was reformed into a residence, with aspects of the building's industrial heritage maintained, such as cast-iron columns and heavy oak beams. Complementing the industrial textures are softer tones in the plasterwork, lime-washed walls, and cement and travertine flooring. The height of the ceilings makes for a grand interior; in the premier bedroom, the lower parts of the wall are painted white, but the original brickwork and beams extend meters above to reveal a water basin manhole. At the end of the bed is an earthenware bathtub, indicating the entrance to the en suite bathroom.

(Above) The top floor of this former brewery once stored grain and hops under a pitched ceiling. Aux bureau removed a section of this roof, leaving the beams, and converted it into a garden terrace.

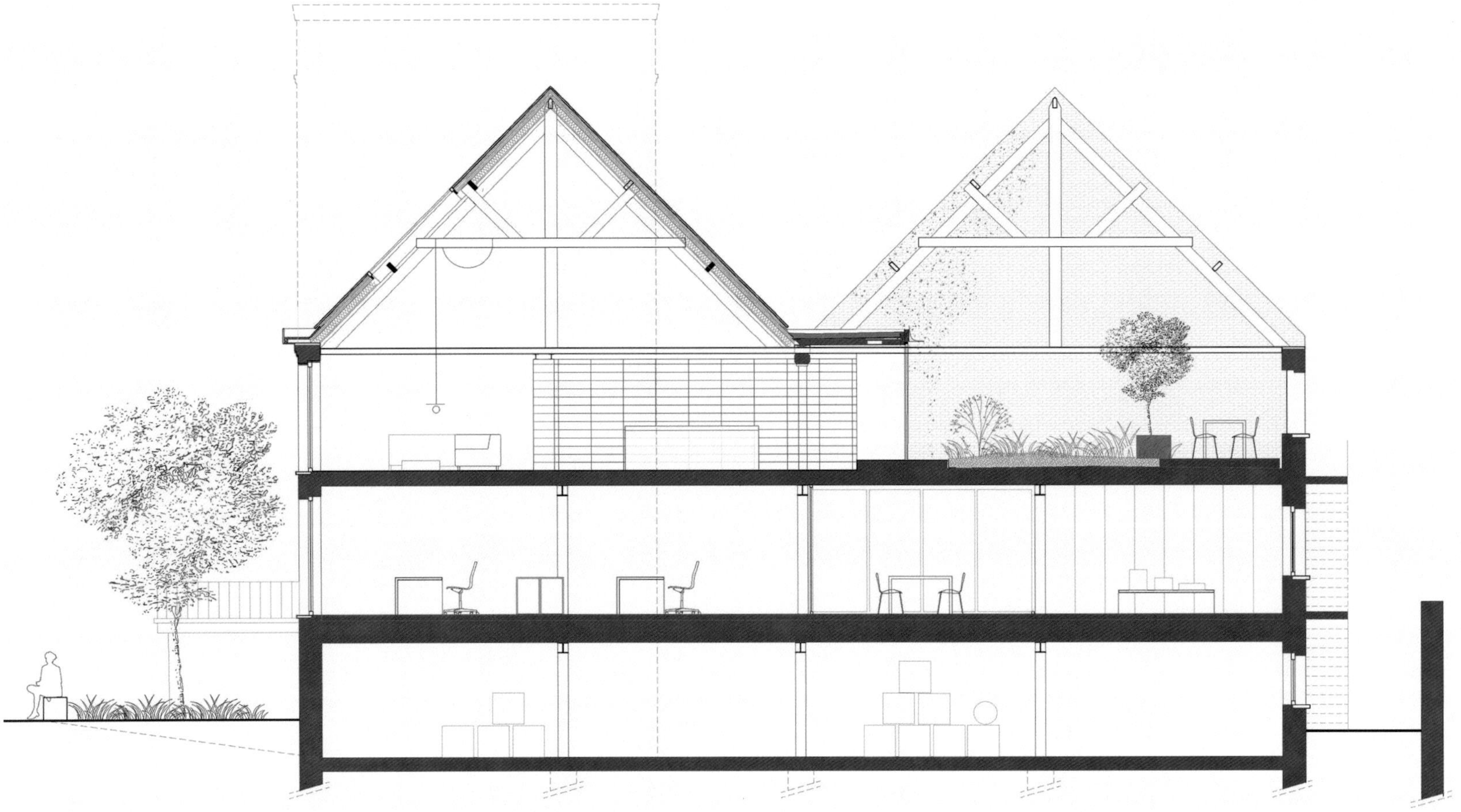

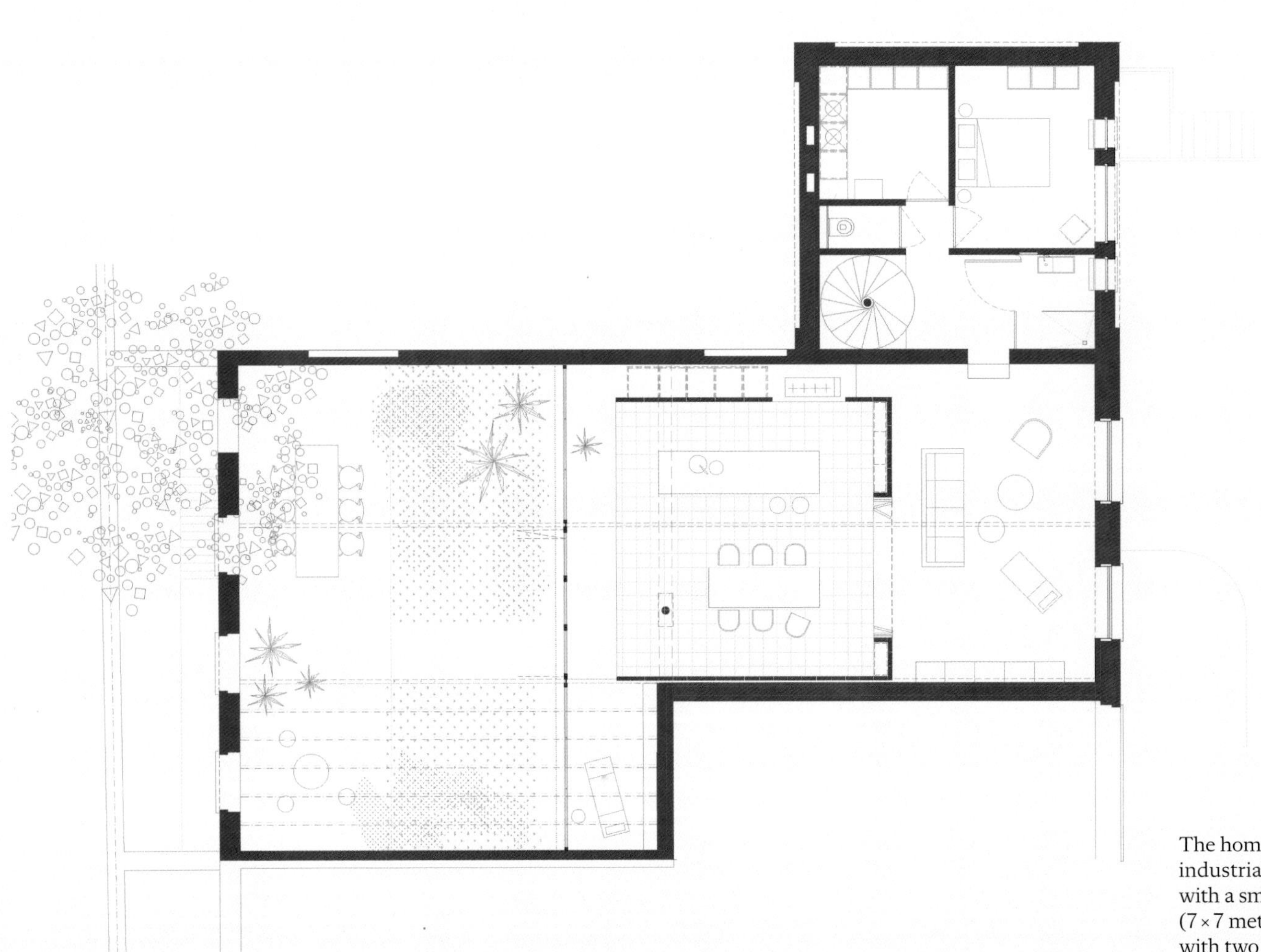

The home was merged from two former industrial buildings: a water tower with a small footprint of 23 × 23 feet (7 × 7 meters) and a three-story brewery with two pitched roofs.

The original timber and steel beams accentuate the impressive height of each room and contrast with the newly plastered soft white walls, travertine floors, and clean decor.

Re/Arrange

Organizing Your Space

One of the most important and effective ways to ensure your home fits your needs is by considering the way your space is arranged. Quality, constructive upgrades can range from rearranging a layout at a macro level to reorganizing furniture within each room.

Build Your Flow

On a larger scale, designing a layout that caters to your day-to-day living habits should be your primary concern. Your house should flow and cohere in a way that makes maximal use of the space and facilitates movement between active areas. To make sure this is the case, rooms should be strategically placed according to function, and they should also optimize your lot space and its surroundings.

Typically, bedrooms are located in the most private, quiet part of a lot, whereas communal areas can be more public-facing and closer to the entrance or garage. Generally, this means that living rooms and kitchens should be placed closer to the street or driveway, while bedrooms will tend toward the sides, back, or upper levels of the house. Consequently, especially in rural and suburban areas, private rooms usually orient toward backyards, tree lines, and other similarly protected zones; in urban areas, where space and privacy are harder to come by, such guidelines may be more difficult to follow. Those with the means to do so may build small yards to distance themselves from adjacent buildings and erect fences. Yet even those without a private outdoor yard will often choose to face primary bedrooms away from the street, preferring exposure to an alley or wall as opposed to a more populated thoroughfare. Such an arrangement will also typically privilege living spaces with better views and natural lighting, whereas the bedroom—the primary function of which is sleep—will feel darker, cozier, and more enveloped. Of course, if privacy is a lesser concern or if the homeowner spends more of their day in their bedroom than the living room, the house's organization should be adjusted as needed.

For homes with multiple bedrooms, the living room and kitchen should be placed in such a way as to be the central hub of activity. Centering these communal spaces fosters sociability among residents, but it also ensures equal accessibility to key spaces from each bedroom. You should never have to cross through private rooms to access other parts of the house (though some intentional exceptions can be made); placing bedrooms around communal and transitory spaces, including hallways, secures privacy and sociability in well-demarcated, separated zones. For families with children, such an arrangement additionally allows parents to keep a watchful eye on children. Though not invariable, this general rule of thumb, followed by most residential designs, has historically been successful in facilitating the flow of a typical household.

Breaking Walls and Building New Ones

If your existing home fails to meet these or other essential spatial requirements, you should consider upgrading your layout. For example, if your home falls drastically short of the number and size of required rooms—a common problem for expanding families—you may consider upgrading with a multi-room addition. Often, these structures horizontally extend from an existing plan, lengthening a hallway and annexing new rooms around it, or affixing additional rooms to the closed edge of a central space, like a living room. With such changes, it is again crucial to consider the overall plan and flow of the home, ensuring that the new wing is accessible and cohesive with regard to the original space.

Some lucky homeowners face the inverse problem: the number of rooms in their house outpaces the number of distinct

(Above) A conspicuous spiral staircase sits at the intersection of the old and new wings of House VDG (see p. 216). (Below) Slim staircases save on space without compromising aesthetic quality in Tokyo's Myougadani House (see p. 196).

(Opposite) Serboli Bureau and Colombo Architecture united multiple elements of the living room, including a sofa, stairs, and planters in a single bespoke masonry unit.

spaces they require for day-to-day living. One of the best and easiest ways to adapt such a layout to new needs is by tearing down walls and cohering distinct areas using furniture. An open plan can make the same area feel larger and more accessible, and it lends the space to unforeseen or changing needs. One of the most common upgrades that home renovators make is combining the kitchen and living room into one open floor plan. Not only do these key areas feel more spacious as a result, but they also become available for larger gatherings and conversations, fostering an air of community. Open floor plans also improve the flow of light and air, especially when windows are limited.

Furnishing

Space upgrades don't have to be as dramatic as adding multi-room structures or tearing down walls. On a smaller scale, making changes to the arrangement of individual rooms can have an enormous impact on your daily life while being relatively easy to do. For owners of small apartments and homes especially, concerted furniture organization is absolutely critical. One way to optimize a small space is to invest in space-saving or multipurpose furniture: hidden kitchens, lofted beds, folding tables, and furniture with built-in storage functions can be a huge help in maximizing your space, and adapting it to the ebb and flow of your day. Otherwise, organizing furniture around zones and focal points can make a small room feel tidier and more intentional, rather than cramped and cluttered.

Focal points can range anywhere from televisions and coffee tables to wall art and windows. Whether small, large, or somewhere in between, every room can benefit from organization around these sites, with sofas and beds oriented to maximize views, and area rugs or well-placed furniture acting as demarcating zones that make a room feel more efficient and organized. To facilitate easy use of each space, renovators should likewise keep pathways of movement in mind. Interior designers typically advocate leaving at least 32 inches (80 cm) of space around furniture to ensure that people have room to walk around with ease. Side tables are a common exception: these should be placed approximately 16 inches (40 cm) from a sofa or recliner for easy access to books and mugs. In general, however, keeping pathways open and accessible will make a space both feel larger and easier to use.

Finally, when rearranging furniture, renovators should always keep lighting in mind. Lighting plays an indispensable role in determining the mood of a room, and can enormously impact the mood of the resident as well. Make sure repositioned furniture still allows light to flow, and optimize lighting where it's most needed—such as on sofas, loungers, and other reading areas. With these organizational tips in mind, owners can substantially upgrade their homes without breaking the bank or severely disrupting their day-to-day living, while those with larger-scale renovations can make use of these recommendations to further perfect their refurbished home.

ANDY WARHOL
Polaroids 1958–1987
TASCHEN

A Heritage-Protected Row House with a Secret Life

HOUSE E+M BY JOSEP FERRANDO ARCHITECTURE
SANT CUGAT DEL VALLÈS, SPAIN
HISTORIC ROW HOUSE → CONTEMPORARY HOME

In a street of row houses in the center of a small town just north of Barcelona sits House E+M. From the quaint and traditional street-facing facade, it is unlikely one could imagine the structure that lies beyond. The cultural heritage of the row house meant that its street-facing facade and roof had to be preserved, but inside, cinder block walls embellished with plywood cabinetry were utilized as the new exterior walls—creating something of a home within a home. Less than 16 feet (5 meters) wide, the residence sits on a complex topographical site between two streets of different heights. The floors themselves are staggered, floating at various heights that overlap each other and reflect the outside landscape. Connecting the floors, a multilevel atrium-like column brings light through the residence, and allows multiple viewpoints of different floors. The exposed plywood leads the materiality, as it makes up much of the interior cabinetry and determines the home's warmth.

(Opposite) Cinder blocks and timber shutters define the back of the house. (Above) Folding french doors open from a wood-clad space onto a balcony overlooking the garden.

(Right and opposite) A grid of timber shelves stretches across all levels along one wall of the residence. The shelving provides much-needed storage throughout the house.

(Above) The arched front door leads into a foyer. Nearby are the kitchen, dining rooms, and the staircase system (above, right) that leads up one side of the house.

PESCA

A Transformation from Bread-Making to Bed-Making

NZ10 RENOVATION BY AUBA STUDIO
PALMA, SPAIN
BAKERY → APARTMENT

A ground-floor bakery in a busy Palma neighborhood has been transformed into a light-filled modern apartment. The back of the building, which previously hosted the bakery's kitchen, was opened and redesigned into a home by Auba Studio. Tiles that originally covered the courtyard were removed, but their mortar remains, creating a 3-D stippled, effect that encourages climbing plants while also dampening noise. Inside, draped lights and exposed wooden beams and pipes give way to the glass ceiling beyond, and large glass sliding doors are all that separate the extension from the exterior courtyard. The glass serves a dual purpose: achieving the coveted "indoor-outdoor" experience to the nth degree, while also increasing illumination in a north-facing space that does not receive direct sun. Inbuilt fir timber furniture runs perpendicular to the courtyard, separating the areas within the home while still allowing light to flow throughout. Polished concrete floors and thick structural beams give weight and permanence to the airy space.

Wooden beams and glazing extend the weather-protected area toward the courtyard while retaining light inside. Large sliding windows seamlessly connect the two zones.

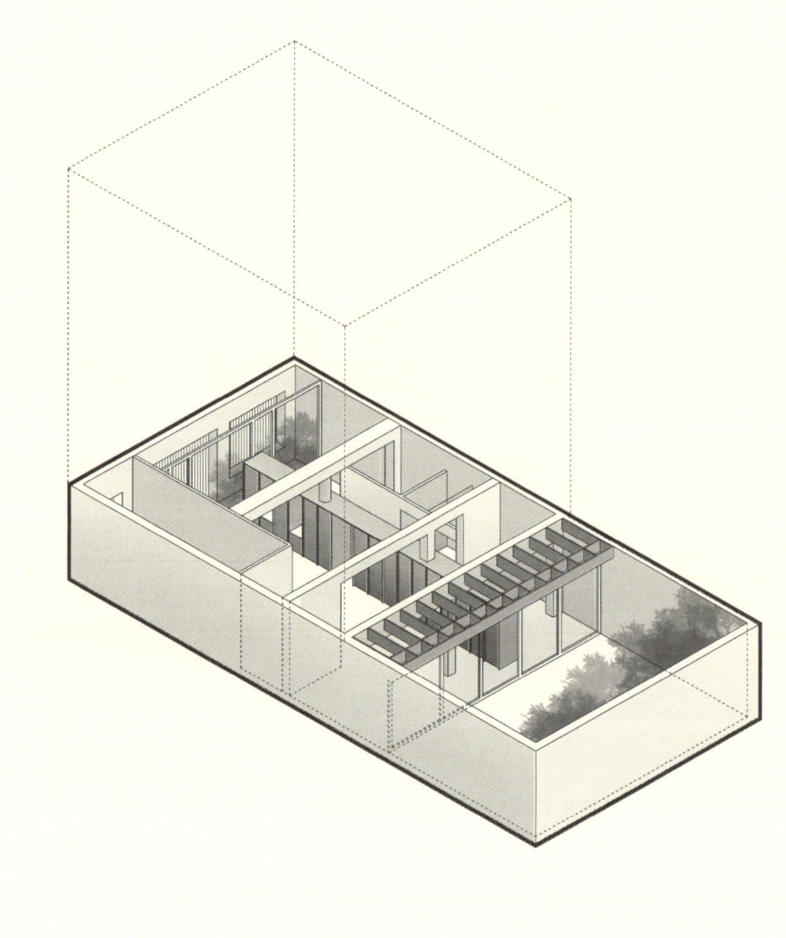

The minimal, calm bedroom can be connected to the terrace by opening the sliding doors, or separated with curtains to create a cozy, private nook.

Light and Dark Meet in a Kyoto Family Home

HOUSE IN SHIMOGAMO BY TD-ATELIER
KYOTO, JAPAN
ABANDONED PROPERTY → REVAMPED FAMILY HOME

House in Shimogamo is idyllically set between a forest-like park and a river on the way to the Shimogamo Shrine in Kyoto. Rather than demolishing the property, which is common for older homes in Japan, the architects refitted the 40-year-old wooden home, taking advantage of its vertical space and reinforcing its earthquake resistance. Now, a slanting vertical wall divides the home into two sides. On the forest side, the wall creates a cave-like space that encourages introspection. Here, where the wall slopes inward as it moves up, is also where the family works and sleeps. On the river side, bright natural light flows in and the wall slants outward toward the ceiling, providing openness in the communal living spaces. The palette is subtle and calming: wooden beams, timber floors, and the dividing wall are paired with white surfaces and minimal aesthetics. The home is now made up of numerous small spaces—suitable for the owners and their various hobbies.

(Opposite) The facade of House in Shimogamo is separated into a light section and a dark section, indicative of the contrasting areas of the interior.

A central diagonal wall separates the home into bright, communal spaces (this page) and darker, more introspective rooms to sleep and work (opposite).

A Statuesque Row House Defined by Timber Accents

THE ROW HOUSE OF WESTERN SUNLIGHT BY YOSHICHIKA TAKAGI + ASSOCIATES
SAPPORO, JAPAN
STUDENT RESIDENCES → FAMILY HOMES

Tall and slim, the Row House of Western Sunlight reaches skywards on its long and skinny "eel bed" Hokkaido block. Despite its thin stature, the home feels spacious with double-height ceilings and copious windows allowing light to flow through and accessing borrowed landscape views from a garden across the street. An earlier illegal extension was removed, and Yoshichika Takagi + Associates reduced the residence from four poorly lit student households with low ceilings to two larger, brighter spaces. The reinforced scrap-lumber frame became a focal centerpiece, visible through large windows from the street. The interior is kept simple, with white walls and pale timber allowing a minimalist backdrop for greenery and cozy furnishings. The architects drew on Scandinavian style for the upper residence, creating a winter living room on the west side of the building. On the top floor, an open rooftop terrace provides outdoor living space for warmer months.

(Opposite) Structural timber beams are revealed to the street through large windows.
(Above) The rooftop terrace is open to the sky, providing ample outdoor living space.

The architects took inspiration from Scandinavian design. Minimal aesthetics, blonde timber, and simple white walls provide a calm backdrop for daily life.

Exterior Facades Become Part of the Interior

RESIDENTIAL EXTENSION IN KANAMACHI BY SO&CO.
TOKYO, JAPAN
COMPACT RESIDENCE → EXPANDED FAMILY HOME

The owner's family had outgrown this small, two-story wooden house in Tokyo and needd an extension. The preexisting bones were maintained, and in some parts, what were once exterior facades have now become part of the interior (with shutter boxes and railings removed). The L-shaped extension increased the space, allowing the family's eldest son a room of his own as he started junior high school. Surrounded by timber, a living room in the center of the first floor evokes a nest-like feel. On one side, a wide staircase leads past bookshelves that cleverly provide structural support to the building. Above, another living space on slatted floors connects it to other spaces in the house. The ground floor was originally oppressively dark, with artificial lighting needed even during the day. To address this, skylights were added, and the timber floor of the mesh-like second level allows light to sift through.

(Opposite) The upper level of the house in Tokyo extends over the level below, and the windows on each floor symmetrically mirror each other.

EVANGELION

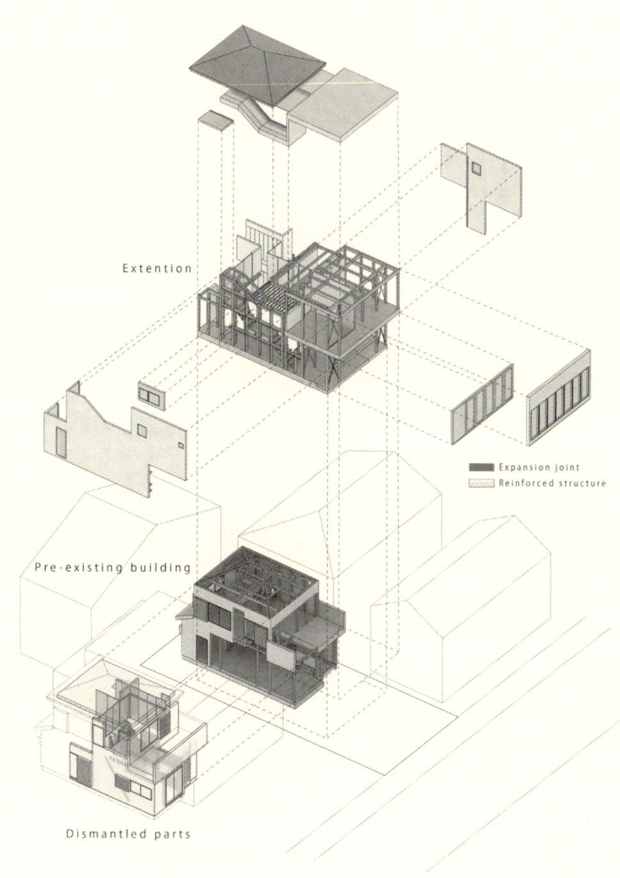

(Opposite) Slatted timber floors allow light from the upper level into the level below. (Right) What was once the exterior facade has now become part of the interior. The exterior was extended to increase living space and to accommodate another room.

A Plethora of Frames as Decorative Collage

K/DOOR HOUSE BY YUTAROU OHTA
GUNMA PREFECTURE, JAPAN
MOUNTAIN RESIDENCE → HOME FOR A COUPLE

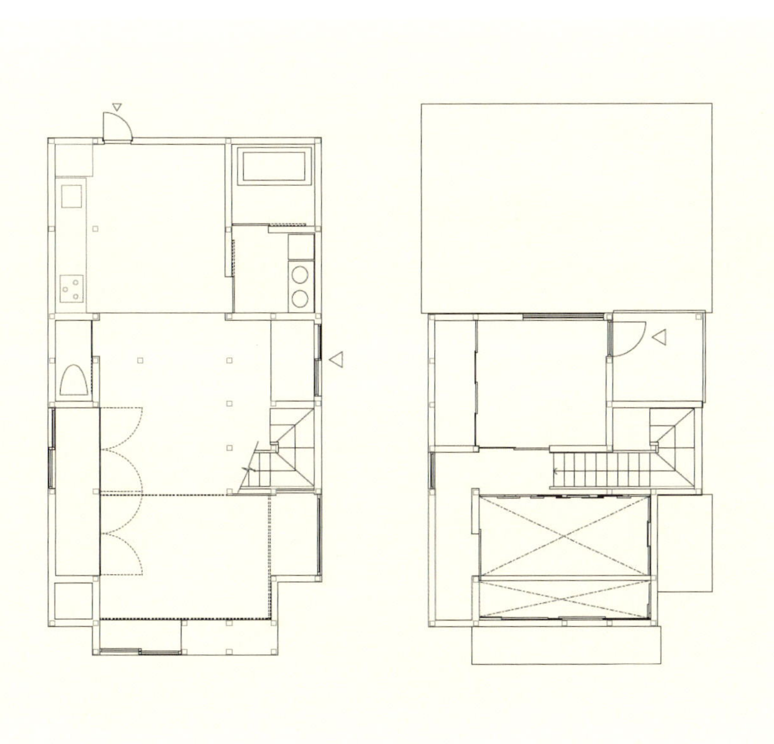

Sage-green frames criss-cross over each other and meld with structural beams and walls in this mountainside home. The house sits in Japan's Gunma Prefecture, set deep in the mountains in a residential community surrounded by a lot of greenery. When a young couple moving from the city purchased the home, it was abandoned and dimly lit, even during the daytime. This absence of light became the starting focal point of the redesign, with the goal of transforming the space into a bright, comfortable haven. The neglected home in the Kanto region of Honshu was stripped, in order to return it to its wooden base. The floor above the living room was also removed to allow light to flow into the space and to create a bright, atrium-style living area. Pastel-green doorways and window frames of various sizes form a gallery-like collage, with walls and handrails as an abstract pattern. Some of the materials used for the home were sustainably repurposed—the stairwell, for example—which reduced the project's footprint.

The materials and color palettes of K/door House are simple, consisting of white plaster and timber structural features, allowing a neutral backdrop for the busyness of the mint-green frames.

(Opposite) Parts of the second level were removed to create a double-height living and study area. The atrium-like space was designed to maximize natural light.

A Farmer's Greenhouse-Like Extension

THE DEFORMED ROOF HOUSE OF FURANO
BY YOSHICHIKA TAKAGI + ASSOCIATES
FURANO, JAPAN
SINGLE RESIDENCE → FAMILY HOME

Named for the irregular structure of its gabled roof, a common style in Hokkaido, the Deformed Roof House of Furano is nestled in a mountainous landscape, with its own asymmetrical crest mirroring the nearby peaks. The owners, a farming couple, extended the residence to allow their son to live separately on the floor above. The architects designed a corrugated, clear polycarbonate extension in order to add external stairs to the main volume, allowing the upper level to be accessed without entering through the ground floor. The transparent frontage reveals timber beams and the facade of the original home. Farmers in the area commonly use the cost effective material for greenhouses, allowing it to blend harmoniously with its context. Before the renovation, the house was disassembled to its frames so as to reform the floorplan, add rooms, increase structural integrity, and improve insulation for the region's cool temperatures. Its interior now features light timber, structural steel beams, and minimal furnishings.

This home's facade is made of polycarbonate, a material commonly used in agriculture. It creates a ghostly shell around the house, partially revealing the skeletal interior structure.

(Opposite) The extension hosts a protected exterior staircase that connects the two households. It contains a terrace and a *doma,* or dirt floor, typical of Japanese farmsteads.

Glow Up

Tips for Lighting Your Home

Lighting can make or break interior design. If you have a home with old or antiquated lights, this reality may have already made itself clear; and even houses with relatively new lighting systems could always benefit from minor refurbishments. Lighting upgrades can improve functionality, lower electricity bills, increase sustainability, and refine a home's style. For homeowners looking to revamp their property, lighting is a great place to start.

Ambient Lighting

Stylistically, well-considered interior and exterior lighting can vastly elevate your home's aesthetics. Interior lighting typically falls into three categories: ambient lighting, accent lighting, and task lighting. Ambient light refers to fixtures that provide general, uniform illumination in a space. Ceiling fixtures are the most common example of this category and may include LED strip lights, recessed lights, flush lights, chandeliers, and more. When upgrading ambient lighting, you should consider the atmosphere generated by the existing lights and adjust as needed. Some homeowners find that their lights are too dim or too harsh, while others may feel dissatisfied with their temperature. When making these changes, be sure not to overcompensate for anything lacking. A common mistake designers make is to under-light small spaces—a tempting route when preset ambient light is perceived as unnecessarily bright. Make sure that your lighting sufficiently reaches corners and nooks—which may require not just stronger lights, but additional fixtures—to achieve a uniform feel. Another solution for harsh lighting is to retrofit lights with dimmers. With adjustable lights, owners can adapt the general atmosphere of their home to different needs at varying times. These fixes will improve the functionality of your home, but they can also refine its overall aesthetic. A spotty, dingy apartment with refitted ambient lights can quickly transform into a well-lit, adaptable, cheery space.

Task Lighting

Task lighting, meanwhile, is exactly what it sounds like: a direct light used for specific tasks. Task lights may include floor and desk lamps, wall-mounted lights in reading nooks, and pendants over an island or kitchen table. Functionally, your task lights should of course be bright and focused (or diffuse) enough to complete the task at hand; when upgrading your task lighting, however, you should consider not only replacing the bulbs, but their shades and frames as well. Editing the style of task lights with new lampshades or pendants can dramatically improve your home's interior design, while the quality of these fittings can even refine the quality of the light itself.

Accent Lighting

Finally, accent lights are an essential complement to decor items, artifacts, art, and accent furniture. These fixtures focus light on a particular area or object, and can include directional wall sconces, floodlights, track lights, and under-cabinet and bookcase lights. If you have items you want to highlight, upgrading your house with accent lights can both bring out the best of the existing design and develop the atmosphere through varied lighting. Mounted artworks, for example, nearly always require special attention: walls tend to receive the least of a room's ambient light, casting an unlit artwork in shadow, but a well-lit wall piece will both draw the eye and brighten the room with color and texture. A focused, directional beam of light will also diversify the tenor of an otherwise ordinarily lit room. Thus, when you update your home, try using a mix of ambient, task, and accent lights to layer and complexify your lighting. This strategy will sophisticate the general ambiance of the interior while improving its functionality—a win on both fronts.

Curate Your Mood

The style of ambient, task, and accent lights can be as unobtrusive or as flamboyant as you like. Well-designed homes include a mixture of both, with an elegant floor lamp, for example, usefully drawing the eye away from a room's less noticeable recessed or strip lights. To upgrade your interior, consider revamping your more conspicuous lighting fixtures by adding a touch of stylistic embellishment. The best way to do this is by selecting an eye-catching design that coheres with the general aesthetic of your home. Chandeliers, metallic bars, art glass, and avant-garde forms beautifully complement modern interior design, while elegant ornaments, faux candles, and dangling crystals lend sophistication to more orthodox homes.

When updating lights, take care to consider the style, function, brightness, and temperature of the new fixtures in tandem with the natural light in the home. Artificial light can beautifully combine with natural sunlight coming in from windows or skylights, while temporarily substituting for it at night. Start by asking, "How bright is the light coming through my windows?" In rooms that don't receive adequate natural light, use lighting to mold the ambiance of the space, mobilizing it to serve both needed functional purposes and to create a soothing atmosphere instead of a shadowy one. In rooms with ample natural light, treat artificial lighting fixtures as task-based supplements or nighttime substitutes. Light, along with color, can have an incalculably powerful effect on both the mood of a room and, as a result, on your own.

Finally, renovators must consider not just style and function, but size and proportion when replacing larger lighting fixtures. An oversized chandelier over a tiny dinner table will make a room feel disproportionate and odd. Take care to make precise measurements of new fixtures and compare them to the room and furniture dimensions; try to visualize how a new light will look and feel in the space. Also, take steps to ensure that new fixtures will mechanically operate within the existing electrical system. In other words, evaluate the plausibility of new lights with aesthetics, functionality, and atmosphere weighed in tandem, as good upgrades can only work with all three.

Outdoor Lighting

Notably, while interior lighting takes precedence in any home renovation, owners should consider upgrading their exterior lighting as well. As with the inside of your home, strive to use a mix of lighting categories outside, using ambient lighting for outdoor seating areas; task lighting for paths, porches, and entryways; and accent lighting for landscaping, architectural details, or water features. Thoughtfully placed exterior lighting will massively elevate your home's curb appeal and provide greater overall visibility, improving safety for you and your guests. To avoid wasting electricity, try retrofitting these lights with motion sensors. This option is a common solution for obvious exterior lighting difficulties while making your home appear more technically advanced. When technology is optimally utilized, the possibilities for functional, stylistic lighting can feel almost endless.

Sustainability

Newer technology can also greatly improve the energy efficiency, and thus cost, of your lighting. Most interior design experts recommend homeowners replace their fluorescent and incandescent light bulbs with LEDs, as the latter have longer lifespans, are safer, and tend to be more sustainable. LEDs are also smaller, which make them more adaptable, and bulbs with the right hardware are easily dimmable. In the vein of new technologies, smart lights are also easier to use and more customizable, allowing residents to turn lights off and on without even leaving their seats. Programmed smart lighting can adapt to the routine of the user without them even pressing a button; many homeowners use smart lighting to help them wake up in the morning or go to sleep at night. If convenience is a priority for you, upgrading your home with smart lighting can have incredible payoffs.

Efficiency, sustainability, cost, and aesthetics all come into play with lighting renovations. If you are planning to refurbish your home, lighting is an essential consideration. A relatively easy adjustment, light upgrades can have powerful effects.

(Above) A trio of corresponding pendant lights hang at varying heights in the Roof House (see p. 134). (Opposite) The low placement of wall sconces in the 18th Street Loft exudes a moody atmosphere while also illuminating the original industrial columns (see p. 52).

Bright Hues Dominate in This 17th-Century Home

VIJZELGRACHT HOUSE
BY BENTHEM CROUWEL ARCHITECTS
AMSTERDAM, NETHERLANDS
WEAVER'S HOUSE → URBAN HOME

From the stately street-facing facade of Vijzelgracht House, it's difficult to predict the vivid, experimental style within. Celebrated Dutch architect Philips Vingboons designed the 17th-century home as a weaver's house. Today it is listed as a national heritage site of the Netherlands. The residence was occupied and used in various ways over the centuries until 2008, and in 2015, the city of Amsterdam declared the structure uninhabitable and fitted it with new foundations. When Benthem Crouwel Architects began designing the intervention in 2017, they approached each room with a keen eye, creating a unique identity for the spaces linked by common threads that run throughout. A floor of warping gray tiles and rafters painted sky blue welcome visitors in the foyer. The colorful ceiling continues into the living area upstairs, except here pale, sage-green rafters complement a cacophony of brightly hued furniture softened by white walls and floors. In the attic, the pitched ceilings are painted yellow and green, contrasting with the chic modern amenities below.

(Opposite) The back of Vijzelgracht House has a starkly modern facade of glass and steel, contrasting with the quintessential brickwork of the surrounding homes and the building's front (above).

A striking iridescent balustrade unites the cacophony of colors seen across the living room, from the yellow handrail and mint roof to the eclectic artworks and multicolored furnishings.

By Name and by Nature: A Home for Dr. Funk

DR. FUNK BY KESSLER PLESCHER ARCHITEKTEN
BUGGENHAGEN, GERMANY
SMALL LAKESIDE COTTAGE → HOLIDAY HOME

Shrouded by trees and a heavy thatched roof, this home by the Baltic Sea has been transformed into a surprisingly light and breezy structure with an interior that is saturated with pastel pops of color. Occupied for over 60 years, the facade and interior surfaces were in bad shape, but the structure and roofing remained intact. The compact floor plan was redesigned for the client—aptly named Dr. Funk—to comfortably host his grandchildren and refresh the decades of deterioration. Light pink and dusty-rose checkerboard tiling is paired with mint-green walls in the living room and kitchen. The latter was expanded to be a large and central communal space. Lightweight pinewood timber is used throughout the communal areas, including on a built-in window seat beside a custom-made neon-yellow dining table overlooking the adjacent lake. Traces of bright yellow follow the woodwork through the kitchen, marking cabinetry touchpoints. This small lakeside cottage is now a sun-drenched, playful family home.

Large windows follow the perimeter of the pink, yellow, and mint kitchen and dining room, providing sweeping views of the lake and harmonizing the interior with the exterior palettes.

Custom furniture and cabinetry made from pinewood panels allow for simple but effective use of space, optimizing the structure's small scale.

A Home within Concrete, Brick, and Steel Walls

TMSN HOUSE BY BLAF ARCHITECTEN
SINT-NIKLAAS, BELGIUM
WAREHOUSE AND RESIDENCE → COWORKING SPACE AND HOME

tmSN House is a coworking space and residence that preserves aspects of the underlying industrial building. A reinvigorated structure and floorplan was built among fragmented brick walls and structural steel beams that remain as indicators of this home's manufacturing history. Built inside a former warehouse and residence with very little open space, the complex was opened up and inverted: what was once the row house residence that abuts the street now hosts the coworking premises, and the adjacent L-shaped warehouse has been converted into a private residence and courtyard.

Within the sturdy structure of concrete, brick, and steel, the internal living spaces are airy and playful, featuring polished concrete floors, light timber accents, and ample windows overlooking the new courtyard. The main living spaces are on the ground floor. On the upper floors, rooms are situated around a central spiral staircase and timber beams corkscrew out from around the stairwell, which begins equidistant to its metal guards.

(Opposite) Patches of paint, vines, and decay cover the external brick courtyard of tmSN House. New masonry was added or entirely removed where damage was irreparable.

Simple furniture proves that beautiful, cost-effective decor is possible, such as the Ikea Tobias chairs seated near a timber dining table and a custom-built timber window bench (opposite).

Reinvigorating and Extending a 1960s Bungalow

HOUSE C-VL BY GRAUX & BAEYENS ARCHITECTEN
DE HAAN, BELGIUM
1960S BUNGALOW → INDUSTRIAL-CHIC RESIDENCE

Situated on a long and narrow plot, this previously "uninspiring" 1960s bungalow was extended and updated into a stylish contemporary residence. Although the original structure was lackluster, the renovation was undertaken with respect for typical Flemish building traditions. Built using sturdy gray stone masonry, the home was doubled in size, becoming three cube structures. Each cube delineates a section of the house, with bedrooms at the front end, dining room and kitchen at back, and the living room in the center. Internally, each room is characterized by a T-shaped support structure that separates zones of the space. These supports are placed differently in each room, allowing for different layouts; in the living room, for example, it hosts a fireplace. Lime-washed stone walls paired with a cream wash on the concrete floor fosters a calm environment. Large recessed windows in the living room allow space for a patio while also increasing the home's connection to the outdoors and creating sight lines between diverse areas.

House C-VL is a masonry home steeped in symmetry and punctuated with large windows. At the back of the house (above), two large sliding-glass doors allow access to the living room and kitchen.

The home's muted palette creates a soft, autumnal aesthetic. In the kitchen, peach pendant lights complement terracotta cabinetry, while the living room features an olive green sofa and lime-washed walls.

SURF TRIBE
THE HISTORY OF SURFING
SURFING
HIGH TIDE
SPECTRUM
The Other Book
SURF SURVIVAL
Surfing Europe
Surfing the World

COTE
2010
2011
GEBOORTEDAG
RELATIES
BE MORE PIRATE

Rural Refresh near the Great Wall of China

THE ROOF HOUSE BY 过半儿 GUÒ BÀN ÉR
BEIJING, CHINA
VACANT PROPERTY → MODERNIZED AND EXTENDED HOME

This rural home, located at the foothills of the Great Wall of China, sat empty for many years before design firm 过半儿 guò bàn ér updated and extended it. "We enjoy giving a vacant house a second life, transforming it from a dwelling with inflexible spaces into a place of active living," says Christian Taeubert, cofounder of the studio. Taeubert applied this philosophy to the Roof House by creating a seamless extension to the existing building. The architects decided to retrofit the existing property rather than to build an entirely new structure. This approach allowed the team to preserve its aesthetic, while sustainably saving on materials and energy. The additional roof makes up a garden-level extension, increasing the living area by 1,290 ft^2 (120 m^2). This creates an intentional split in levels between the dining and living rooms, and connects the living area to the timber deck and the garden. The interior hosts a minimal, predominantly white palette, enhanced with features such as a wide fireplace and rustic furniture that reference the home's countryside location.

(Opposite) The architects created new areas by extending the roof, which now provides shelter and shade in the garden.

The architects devised an airy space that allows flexibility for a large range of activities. The concrete roof pitches up at the east and west sides to lodge a tea room (opposite) and a spa.

Restroom Renovation

Upgrading an Intimate Space

The bathroom, like the kitchen, has to marry aesthetic concerns with functionality and efficiency, requiring bathroom-specific appliances and storage solutions to cohere with the general aesthetic of a home. When upgrading your bathroom, first evaluate how your needs could be better met. Are you low on storage space? Do you have trouble cleaning or draining appliances? Does your restroom adequately vent? Do you wish you had more settings on your shower, toilet, or sink, or do you wish you had more bathroom fixtures altogether? If you're satisfied in all the above departments—is there anything you would add or change about your restroom's cosmetics?

To preface, always consult an expert before beginning an invasive bathroom renovation. Plumbing systems are no joke, and neither is water damage or odor—two issues that can arise from faulty refurbishments. The effort and funds required to hire a consultant will always be preferable to falling victim to a costly mistake down the line.

The Toilet

Let's start with the primary fixture in every bathroom: the toilet. This daily-use appliance should above all be functional, easy to clean, and comfortable. If you have trouble scrubbing your toilet, face frequent clogs, or are dissatisfied with the seat's comfort, consider replacing the fixture with a newer model that works as needed. If you're looking for something more luxurious, try adding a bidet seat to your existing toilet or substituting it with a new bidet toilet entirely. These fixtures feature spraying a jet of water outward from inside the bowl, and they often come with customizable settings for temperature, water pressure, nozzle position, and spray width. A few are self-cleaning and specifically designed to minimize odor. Some bidets additionally have heated toilet seats, while renovators with a lower budget can purchase a component heated toilet seat for attachment to their existing fixture. The options for toilet customization are surprisingly diverse, and homeowners should determine if they want an added dose of opulence for the porcelain seat.

The Shower

Showers, too, can come in a great deal of forms and styles, with luxury options affording additional customization. If you plan to renovate your shower, start by thinking about its shape: is it a walk-in shower, or a bathtub/shower combination? If you currently own the latter and have the means, is it a priority for you to separate your shower and bath—a typical step for homeowners aiming to upgrade their bathroom to the next level?

Any type of shower will benefit from a storage shelf: more affordable options include hanging caddies and soap dishes, while homeowners looking for a ritzier look might opt for a recessed niche. If you have a walk-in shower or plan to install one, consider adding a bench, which not only makes your bathroom more accessible, but also allows you to rest as you rinse off.

Other shower upgrades can be comparatively less invasive. Many people enjoy listening to music in the shower, but running water will often overpower a song, especially if you are listening from a lower-quality speaker, like your phone. Installing a well-made shower speaker will vastly improve your listening experience—and your long showers as a result. These speakers can also be quite cheap, costing around the range of a regular Bluetooth speaker. In contrast, faucet and lighting upgrades are typically priced higher, but they can also have far more dramatic effects.

If you have the time and money to do so, updating your showerhead or even adding additional ones can make your experience feel fun and extravagant. Rainfall and waterfall shower heads, which have greater and more uniform coverage, will give you a more consistent warm feeling; handheld shower heads are more functional, allowing you to wash harder-to-reach parts of your body with ease; filtered shower heads can be healthier for your skin and hair, reducing the amount of chlorine and hard water in your shower; and steam showers, which admittedly require far more substantial modifications

Playful elements give bathrooms character, such as Point Supreme Architects' use of nautical references and the color blue (above, see p. 66), and the ball-foot tub by Andrée Putman and Marie-Anne Derville in the iconic Hôtel d'Hallwyl (below).

(Opposite) At the foot of the bed in this steam-brewery conversion, a tub marks the entrance to an en suite bathroom. The ceilings extend high above and feature original brickwork (see p. 70).

than a simple faucet replacement, bring a veritable sauna into the comfort of your home. Some showerhead types are compatible with others, classified as dual showerheads. These fixtures commonly refer to showerheads that can oscillate between handheld and fixed, but even some rainfall showers can toggle between rainfall settings and normal fixed settings. If you are considering renovating your shower, upgrading your showerhead will often be the most obvious and effective step, effectuating clear improvements with little change.

The Tub

Buying a new bathtub can also dramatically improve your restroom experience in terms of both style and function. Free-standing bathtubs are what most people think of when they imagine a luxury bathroom. These tubs are not connected to any walls or other surfaces (save for the floor), meaning they require a lot of space and square footage. Free-standing tubs are perfect for homeowners who love a deep soak, or who have beautiful views and interiors they want to revel in or show off. The only downside to this style is its exposed plumbing, but an experienced designer will be able to celebrate and capitalize on this unique feature rather than suffer from it. In fact, a free-standing tub with exposed plumbing will often conform perfectly to an industrial, rustic, or vintage-style bathroom; the classic clawfoot tub, for example, is a mainstay of vintage interior design.

Drop-in bathtubs are another example of luxurious, spacious tub design, referring to fixtures that fit into a prepared bathroom deck. These tubs leave you more than enough space to rest your toiletries, towels, clothes, and a book nearby, while the covered deck space can afford additional storage or more advanced tub settings, such as jacuzzi streams. These types of tubs are easier to integrate into a cohesive bathroom design—decks can extend the tiling of your walls or floor—but they also tend to be more expensive, especially because they require further construction and customization. The cheapest and most common bathtub style is the alcove tub, which sits within a three-sided enclosure and often comes as a tub and shower combination, thereby saving space. The traditional use of these tubs shouldn't stop you from making them luxurious, however: drop-in bathtubs can be installed in an alcove, and the alcoves themselves can be designed around windows or with custom lights, making them a visual focal point of the bathroom. Depending on your needs, budget, and space, select the bathtub that makes the most sense for you and for the interior design.

The Sink

Finally, bathroom sink styles range across a wide variety of options, including wall-mounted sinks, which protrude horizontally from a wall; pedestals, where bowls are mounted on a column; drop-in and under-mounted sinks, which recess below a countertop; vessel sinks, which sit atop the counter; trough sinks, which are wide, deep, and resemble, well, a trough; and more. Each of these options cater to different preferences

and needs: while wall-mounted sinks and pedestals can clear up extra foot space in your bathroom, sinks with countertops afford more storage opportunities and easier access to your toiletries. Vessel sinks, pedestals, and wall-mounted sinks are aesthetically pleasing and sometimes—especially in the case of vessels—downright eye-catching. However, trough sinks can be more functional, especially if multiple people share one restroom. Installing two sinks in a bathroom, if space allows, also provides more functionality for multiple users.

In sum, when renovating your bathroom, evaluate the number of people who will share the room, consider your storage needs, think about the existing design, and make a decision from there. It will help as well to make decisions about each of your bathroom fixtures and furniture items in tandem; for example, purchasing a towel bar or rack, medicine cabinet, or floating shelving for the restroom can alleviate the need for sink-based storage. While it would be easy to make individual decisions about each isolated fixture, renovating—and designing in general—is a delicate act of balancing varying needs and wants. The most successful upgrades will always keep this dictum in mind.

The Design

Of course, cosmetics have to be a part of this balancing act, and as with general functionality, it has to be considered with all elements of the space in mind. Successfully designed bathrooms will contain varied but harmonious patterns, colors, and materials across the walls, cabinetry, floors, tiling, and—if present—shower curtains and bath mat. Think especially about the cohesion of the metal finishings and how they complement (or don't) the rest of the design. While most restrooms will use ceramic or porcelain for tubs and sinks and stainless steel for faucets, some of the most stunning vintage, farmhouse, and rustic-style bathrooms benefit from beautiful copper finishings and tubs. As is the case in any room, renovators should also use layered lighting, including over tubs and in showers, on the rims of mirrors, and even over the toe kicks of cabinets, if possible. These supplements, combined with luxurious functional additions such as heated flooring and entertainment centers, will offer the final touch to your dream bathroom renovation.

Open-air bathrooms—or bathrooms with a connection to the outdoors—remain popular in luxury design. Hé! Architectuur's Karper House (above, see p. 152) features a bathtub overlooking an outdoor terrace.

A Light and Airy Vacation Home in Barcelona

ROCHA APARTMENT BY SERBOLI BUREAU AND COLOMBO ARCHITECTURE
BARCELONA, SPAIN
NEGLECTED APARTMENT → VACATION HOME

Desirably located between two of Barcelona's busiest squares, Rocha Apartment is a breezy nook that feels far from the heart of the city. Serboli Bureau and Colombo Architecture redesigned the apartment to update the once-neglected space and its inadequate floor plan. Now, the vacation home features clean white lines, simple furnishings, gray microcement floors, and open spaces. Rooms are delineated with white-painted metal frameworks, with one suggesting an entrance foyer at the front door. Tiling in the en suite bathrooms is brightly colored, connected again by the open framework that allows the bathrooms to be subtly separated from the bedrooms. The exterior patio, which was restored, is extended to connect with an indoor conversation circle. The zones are only partially demarcated by a large window that opens between the two, but *rasillas,* or long thin bricks, run between the spaces, unifying the indoors and outdoors and seamlessly connecting the home to the outside world.

This Barcelona apartment features typical Catalan vaulted ceilings, terracotta tiles, and an alluring terrace. Much of the apartment was painted white, creating a calm environment.

(Opposite) Terracotta-hued tiles determine an indoor-outdoor terrace zone. The terrace has copious seating for entertaining and provides the option to be protected from the sun.

Each bedroom delivers a significant pop of color at the entrance to the en suite bathrooms. One features peppermint-green tiles and paint, the other buttercup yellow.

An Adaptable Residence in a Former Warehouse

KARPER BY HÉ! ARCHITECTUUR
BRUSSELS, BELGIUM
INDUSTRIAL BUILDING → RESIDENCE AND STUDIO

Renewable, simple, and raw materials contribute to the overall palette and calm tonality of Karper, named for the building's location on Karperstraat in Brussels. Hé! Architectuur designed the home in a former workshop and warehouse using natural materials to minimize CO_2 emissions, including a timber exposed-beam roof extension, straw bale, cork and lime hemp insulation, and clay plaster and rammed earth walls. The simplicity of the materials creates a somewhat rustic and homey escape—a contrast to the dense, urban context of the Belgian capital. The architects sought to increase housing density to adapt to the city's exponential growth without cutting corners on green space. To achieve this, a new roof deck capitalizes on the benefits of building vertically, providing a rare and much-desired garden space. Double-height windows lead from the white-tiled deck into the living room, allowing light to spill inside. The architects placed the living spaces on the top floor to prioritize luminosity and privacy. The home is proudly "low-tech," providing a pared-back and timeless structure.

(Opposite) The exterior facade integrates with the surrounding buildings in both materiality and color. (Above) A sunny terrace provides sunshine and planters for greenery.

(Opposite) Double-height windows lead from the living room to the terrace, allowing copious light into the apartment. (Above) The kitchen was placed on the upper level to capture more luminosity.

Lime-washed walls, timber accents, floor-to-ceiling curtains, and soft furnishings ensure that this former warehouse space feels homey and welcoming rather than stark and industrial.

Upcycling
Upcycling

An Industrial Space Imbued with Rustic Charm

10AM LOFTS BY STUDIO ANDREW TROTTER,
GAVALAS IOANNIDOU ARCHITECTURE, AND EVA PAPADAKI
ATHENS, GREECE
INDUSTRIAL BUILDING → LOFTS AND EVENT SPACE

Emanating brutalist minimalism with a hint of rustic charm, this former 1970s industrial building in the downtown neighborhood of Gazi, in Athens, was transformed into six lofts, an event space, and a penthouse. The ground floor and basement were gutted to make way for the venue space and accentuated with black cement floors and stark white walls, then tempered by curving staircases, original raw concrete, worn timber, and creamy textiles and linens. Glass bricks replace a large ground-floor wall, allowing diffuse natural light to soften the dark base of the building and to illuminate a hefty antique dining table. The penthouse brims with a sense of rough luxury: painted lime-plaster walls complement heavy, flaxseed-hued linen curtains and tailored ceramics and sculptures by the likes of Yiorgos Trichas. Minimalist aesthetics and heirloom furniture blend with acclaimed designs; Charlotte Perriand *Dordogne* chairs stand close to ancient Greek pottery, and a Pierre Jeanneret rattan bench sits by the spiral concrete staircase in the foyer.

(Opposite) The exterior of 10AM Lofts exudes brutalist charm. (Above) A large dining table surrounded by Charlotte Perriand Dordogne chairs sits beside a new wall of glass bricks.

(Opposite) The light and airy ground floor venue space is rentable for events, exhibitions, and creative purposes. It features a spiral concrete staircase that leads to the mezzanine level.

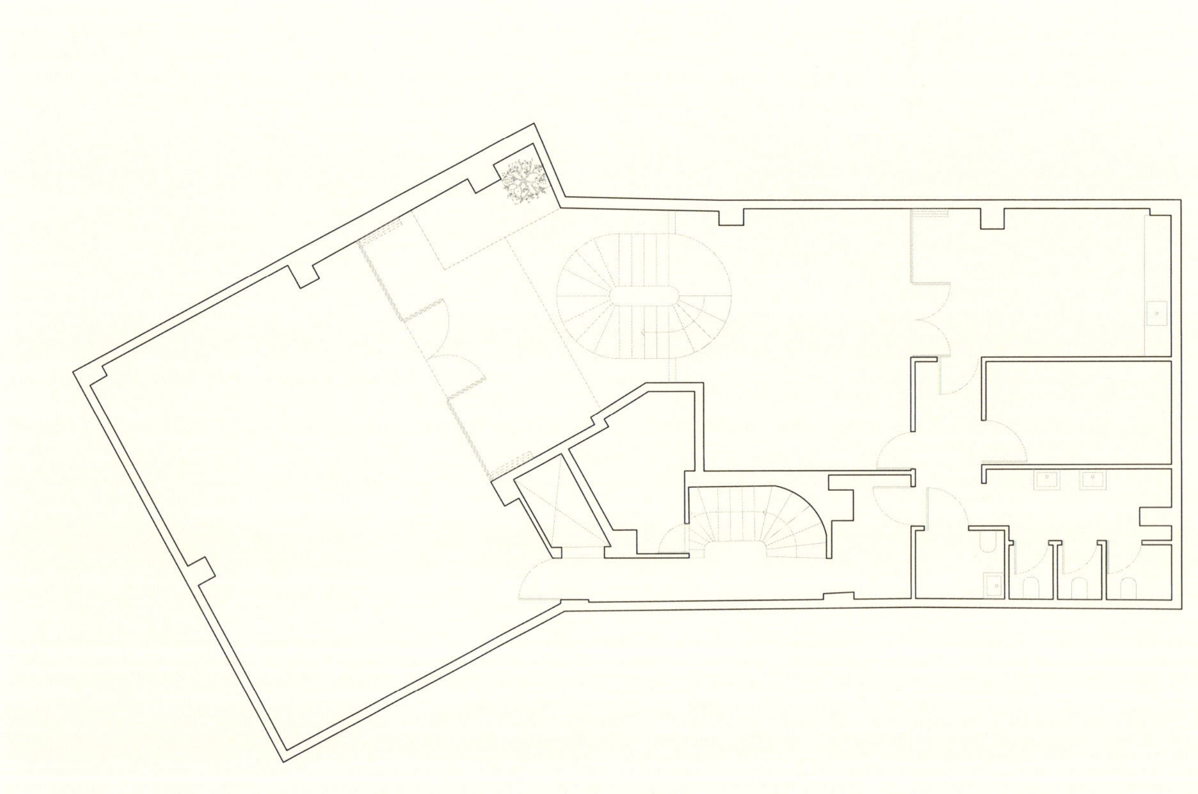

(Above, right) One bathroom beside the rooftop terrace features a large stand-alone bathtub with stunning views over the city. The penthouse has a dark, sensuous, and luxurious palette.

A Modern Intervention on a Countryside Home

MADE OF SAND BY STUDIO WEAVE
AXMINSTER, U.K.
COTTAGE → VACATION HOME & ARTIST RETREAT

On the site of a historic local sandpit, Made of Sand is a two-story red cedar–clad extension to a secluded cottage in Devon, England. The architects replaced a neglected garage and workshop that were in a serious state of disrepair with a guesthouse and creative space. The space is self-contained, and connected internally through a shared antechamber and to the exterior via a restored stone staircase. The extension does not aspire to imitate the original structure of the house. Rather, it is boldly modern against its historic backdrop, choosing only to reference the color of the original slate roof and the surrounding landscape. Inside, a cocoon-like living area is framed in custom Douglas fir paneling and shelving, opening to a window looking out on the countryside greenery. Additional materials further the warm tonality, including brass, softly curving clay walls, and terracotta. Additionally, the thermal performance of the old building was improved to minimize its footprint.

(Left) While one side of the building retains its original style, the new guesthouse provides an engrossing contrast in color, shape, materiality, and even window size.

This cozy living area in the new guest wing is clad in Douglas fir. The warming timber is used for shelving, storage, and to create a cocoon-like atmosphere.

Nature Embellishes This Brickwork Extension

BD HOUSE BY SPACE ENCOUNTERS
BERGEN, NETHERLANDS
1950S HOME → NATURE-INFUSED FAMILY VILLA

Due to its characteristic charms, a young family decided to renovate and extend this modest villa—which was no longer fit for contemporary use—rather than demolish it. The original shape remains, with its peaking red-tiled roof and white facade, but now an extension at the back of the home references the iconic Swedish architect Sigurd Lewerentz through dark brickwork and contrasting white grouting, which created a striking pattern. A large circular hole in the veranda's cantilevered roof leaves space for a tree to grow, merging nature with the structure. This circular void marks the center of the grounds, intrinsically connecting the home with the surrounding garden and maritime trees. Large sliding doors framed with *Fraké* wood allow for seamless flow between the garden and interior, leading into the new primary bedroom and living room. Inside, rectangular tiles in the kitchen mimic the shape of the exterior brickwork and are paired with timber cabinetry, soft accents, and terrazzo floors that flow through the home.

(Opposite) BD House merges with nature—plants spill over its roofline and trickle down its walls. In the center of the terrace, a tree grows through a circular rift in the bricks.

The young owners originally wished to demolish the villa, but after living in it for a few weeks, they decided to renovate instead and maintain the roofline of the original building.

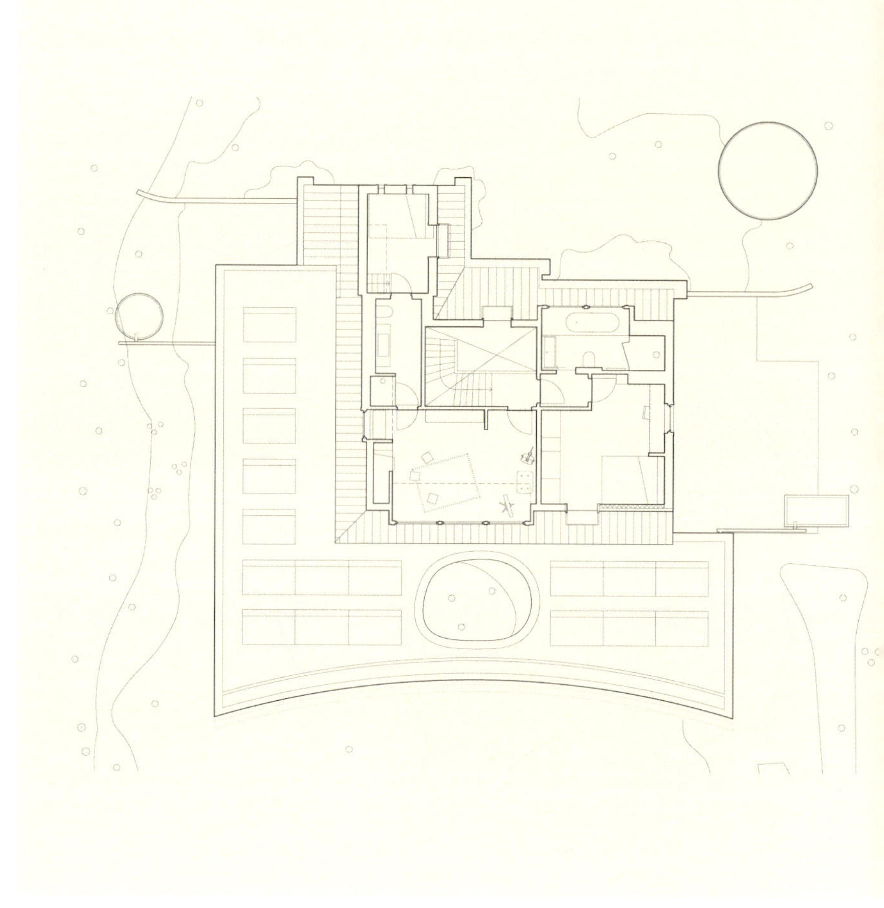

The modest primary bedroom is located on the ground floor. Its large sliding windows open to the garden and a curving brick patio.

A Wartime Prison Transformed into a Home

HOUSE OVER THE WALL BY CHAOFFICE
BEIJING, CHINA
WARTIME PRISON → COURTYARD HOME

With a courtyard that was destroyed during World War II and rebuilt as a temporary wartime prison, House over the Wall holds a wealth of history. After the war, the home was returned to its owners and eventually abandoned for decades. Its partially collapsed state left the architects considering an entire rebuild, but the privacy offered by the high courtyard walls was too alluring to give up. Opting instead to renovate, the clients' relatively low budget left the question of how to best preserve the historic atmosphere while optimizing space. The home now merges aspects of the locale's quintessential historic design—featuring traditional roof tiling, stonework, and the original structural supports—with modern touches such as polished concrete aggregate floors, sleek dark timber, clean white walls, and strengthening steel structural supports. To increase light in the former dark and gloomy interior, skylights and tiered windows were added to illuminate the spaces while retaining coveted seclusion.

(Opposite) The high courtyard perimeter of House over the Wall is a remnant from its history as a prison. Today, the walls forge a private space hidden from busy urban surroundings.

(Above) The house sat abandoned for decades, becoming dilapidated and overrun with plants. Chaoffice rebuilt and strengthened the almost-collapsed building with a new steel structure.

The original structure was very dark, with only the courtyard receiving light. New structures were attached to the roof and walls to increase light and airflow.

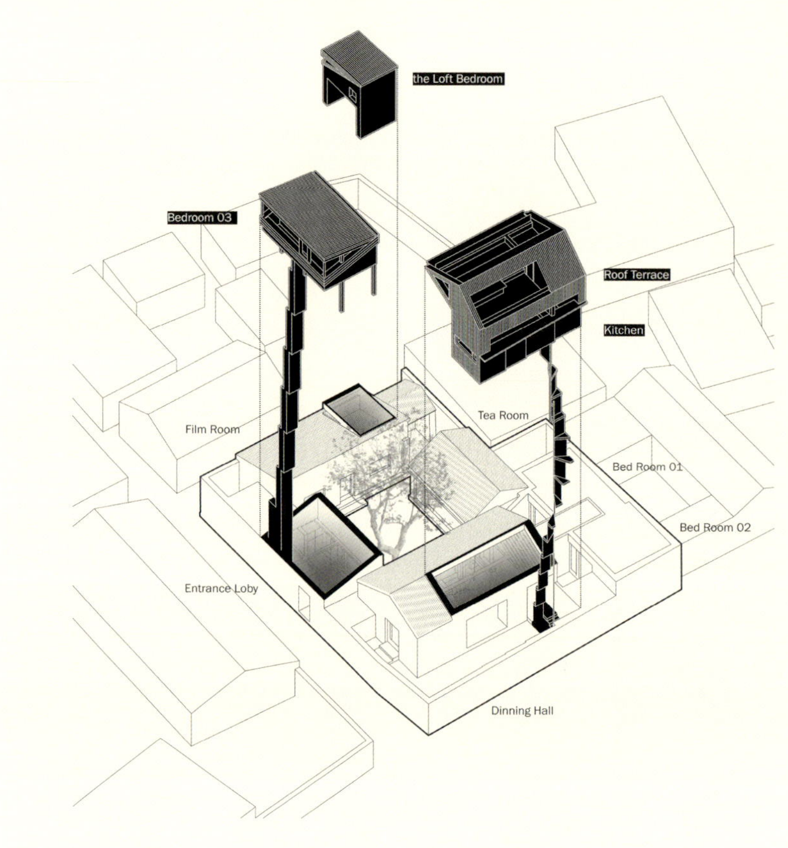

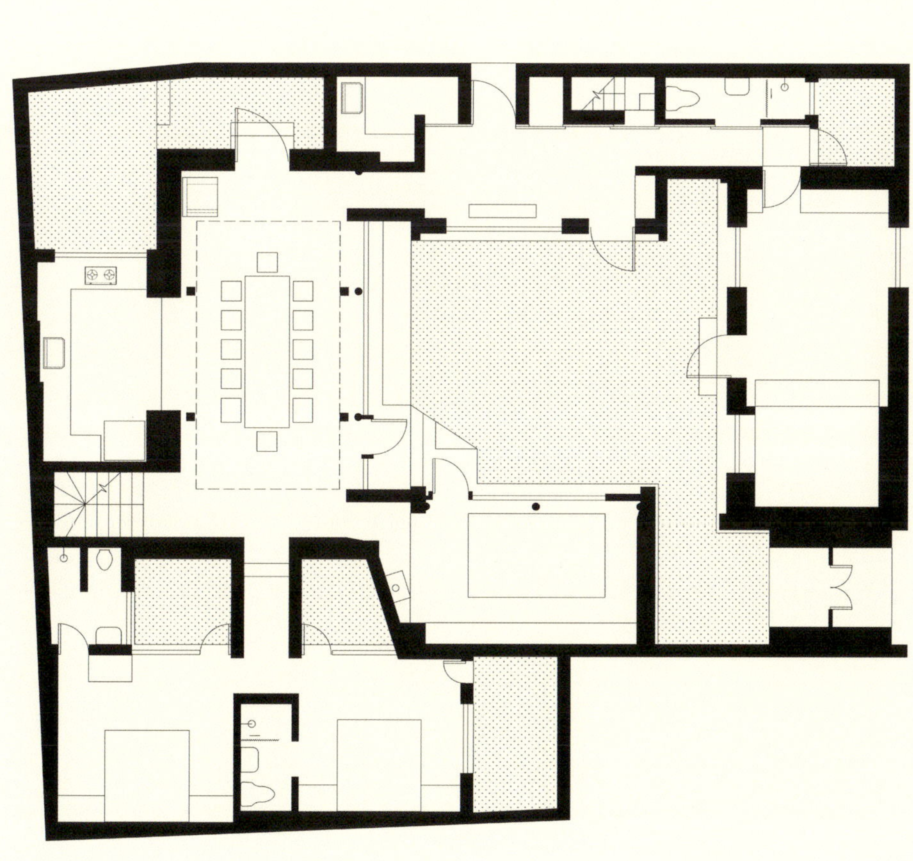

Designing for Cooking

Renovate Your Kitchen

Kitchen renovations can be broadly divided into three categories: layout updates; appliance overhauls and other functional improvements; and cosmetic enhancements.

The Kitchen Work Triangle

Updating the arrangement of your kitchen is the most invasive of these processes, but if your home comes equipped with a poorly designed or otherwise inefficient kitchen, renovating the layout can create dramatic change. When upgrading your kitchen plan, start by considering how you typically use the space. In particular, if you are an avid home chef, try to modify the layout to be more efficient according to your standard food preparation and cooking sequence. Most interior designers recommend breaking down the components of a kitchen into three focal points (colloquially termed the kitchen "work triangle"): the refrigerator, the sink, and the stovetop/oven. These zones should be close (but not too close) to improve the efficiency of food preparation and eliminate wasted steps. While the organization of the work triangle should still allow for a great deal of variation and customization, designers recommend the following guidelines:

1) The perimeter of the triangle should range between 13 and 26 feet (4 to 8 meters).
2) Each element—the refrigerator, sink, and cooktop—should extend between 4 and 9 feet apart (1 ¼ to 2 ¾ meters),
3) Avoid obstacles in the immediate kitchen triangle pathway, such as islands, cabinets, bar carts, and tables. (For example, while an island can and often does sit comfortably in the center of the work triangle, it should not seriously obstruct the lines of movement between each appliance.)

These guidelines will improve the flow and efficiency of your kitchen experience, and ensure that it prioritizes functionality while remaining broad enough to allow for personalized variations and space constraints. Sometimes, space permitting, renovators will elect to double an element—adding a second sink to their island, for example—for even greater practicality. Homeowners should first and foremost consider their own needs when rearranging their kitchen layout and adapt the work triangle to their preferred cooking process. As these design guidelines show, however, any significant layout change should be preceded by a rigorous planning process, including a careful measurement of dimensions. While this requirement may initially seem onerous, the final result will almost always make up for the expended effort.

Appliance Upgrades

Once the overall plan has been determined, or even if you don't intend to make considerable changes, upgrading your kitchen appliances and making other functional improvements is an obvious step. These updates may extend to sinks, refrigerators, cooktops, microwaves, countertops, drawers, cabinets, and more. The sink is a fantastic example of how a simple appliance upgrade can dramatically elevate your cooking process. Many high-end kitchen sinks on the market are specifically designed to facilitate food preparation, coming equipped with pull-down faucets; multiple spray settings (including ring sprays, sweep sprays, soft sprays, and various water pressure options); built-in drying racks, cutting boards, and strainers; double bowls; and even additional faucets. These options not only make cooking more efficient, but they also save counter space around the sink. Homeowners should likewise reevaluate the material of their kitchen sink, with stainless steel being the most popular for its stain- and heat-resistant qualities. However, conscientious renovators may choose other materials, including copper, enamel, cast iron, ceramic, composite, or other options for aesthetic reasons. A stainless-steel sink may look out of place in an otherwise traditionally designed interior, whereas copper can lend an air of luxury and functionality while blending seamlessly with a farmhouse-style home, for example.

Refrigerator upgrades are another useful change to make: luxury refrigerators may come with surprisingly practical amenities, including automatic ice makers, chilled water

Careful tile selection enhances kitchen aesthetics. Dusty-rose and pink tiles bring a playfulness (above, see p. 120), while slim white tiles mirrored in the kitchen walls and table anchor the design (below, see p. 22).

(Opposite) The kitchen of Myougadani House sits beside a light well in the frame of a former staircase, encouraging plant growth. The island element is moveable, which allows the setup to evolve as needed (see p. 196).

dispensers, increased freezer space, efficacious shelving (including humidity-controlled drawers for fruits and vegetables), and more. Renovators with a lower budget or less space should consider upgrading their refrigerator with whichever of these amenities they will find most useful. The same suggestion can extend to other appliance upgrades, such as cooktop and microwave replacements.

Install a Backsplash

One of the most common recommendations for kitchen renovations includes installing a backsplash if your home does not already have one. While not strictly necessary in the same way a stove or a sink is, a backsplash will provide much-needed protection from grease, smoke stains, and water, which can damage and discolor your walls. A backsplash should be made of a durable, nonabsorbent, and easily cleanable material, such as tile, quartz, marble, metal, glass, granite, and more. Usefully, backsplashes can also provide an aesthetic pop to your kitchen, and many homeowners unfamiliar with the concept may assume it exists for purely stylistic reasons. Make sure to match the color and material of your backsplash to the general aesthetic of your kitchen, which should read harmonious and cohesive. A modern white and gold marble backsplash, however beautiful, may not be the best choice for an industrial or rustic kitchen style.

Kitchen Organizing

Perhaps the easiest and simplest kitchen upgrade one can make is adding accessories and organizers for improved functionality. Most homeowners use utensil organizers for their drawers, but those attuned to their standard cabinet use may find additional organizers fruitful as well. Pot racks and plate racks for walls allow you to show off beautiful silverware while facilitating ease of access, and adding additional cabinets or carts can increase limited storage space. These upgrades are comparatively cheap and easy to install, and if your space allows, consider making this simple change.

Cooking in Style

Last, but certainly not least, cosmetic concerns should always accompany any larger change made to your kitchen, from layout rearrangement to appliance replacements to entirely new installations. Think about the design aesthetic of the rest of your home and how best to match your new kitchen to that existing template. Many kitchens require materials not used in most other rooms, including countertops, backsplashes, and appliances; these should blend into your original aesthetic while remaining stylistically pleasing on their own. Remodelers can repaint cabinets, install new lights (including pendant and under-cabinet lights), add decor, and consider proportions to ensure that efficiency concerns do not sacrifice style. When it comes to utilitarian spaces like the kitchen, form and function do not have to be a dichotomy, with one coming at the expense of the other. The best designers and renovators will adequately account for both.

Pigmented Cement Pops in This London Terrace

THE HOUSE RECAST BY STUDIO BEN ALLEN
LONDON, U.K.
VICTORIAN TERRACE → RETIREMENT HOME

The House Recast by Studio Ben Allen is a captivating Victorian terrace in north London, noteworthy for its innovative use of concrete and color. The home's owners approached the design studio and encouraged experimentation on the property—which allowed project leaders Omar Ghazal and Ben Allen to work with off-site fabrication, a technique often underutilized in smaller projects. The architects chose pigmented patterned concrete as a stalwart feature of the home. The concrete is both structural and aesthetic, inspired by the decorative and load-bearing qualities of the area's Victorian-era brickwork. Color radiates from the house; one bathroom features green concrete, an arched ceiling, and bespoke fixtures and fittings that evoke a hammam. A blue CNC-cut balustrade mirrors the home's front facade pattern, while the kitchen benches are a cheerful orange. Studio Ben Allen created a home that is eclectic, beautiful, and exudes a sense of joy for the owners in their retirement.

(Opposite) Color reigns in this mischievous home. A green cross splits the back facade into four. The top right features a block of burnt-orange, contrasting with the historic brickwork.

(Left) Louvered vaulted ceilings bring diffused light into the kitchen. The bright, burnt-orange kitchen countertops the color on mimic the rear exterior and nearby steps.

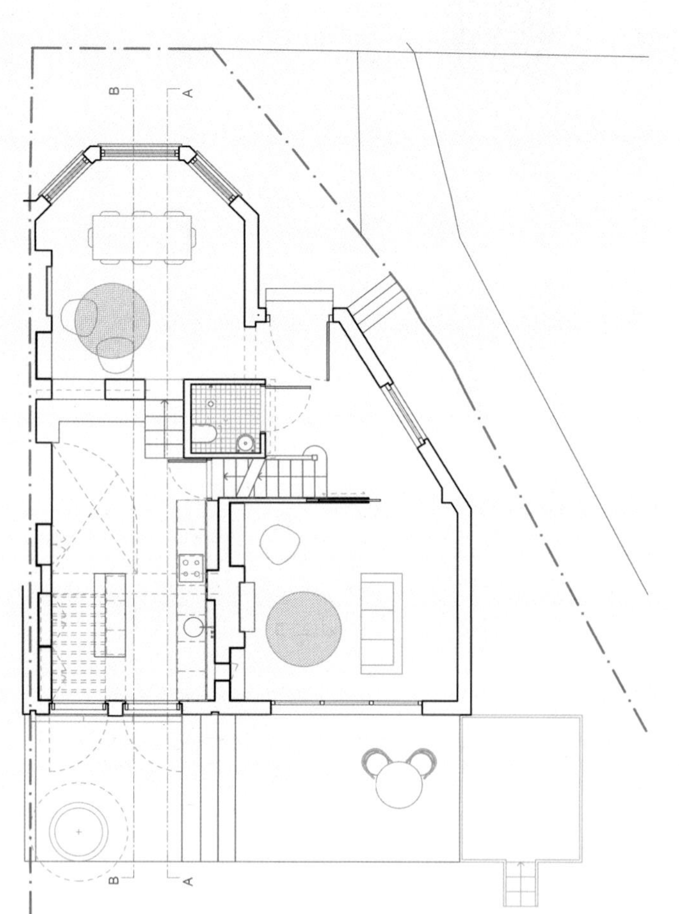

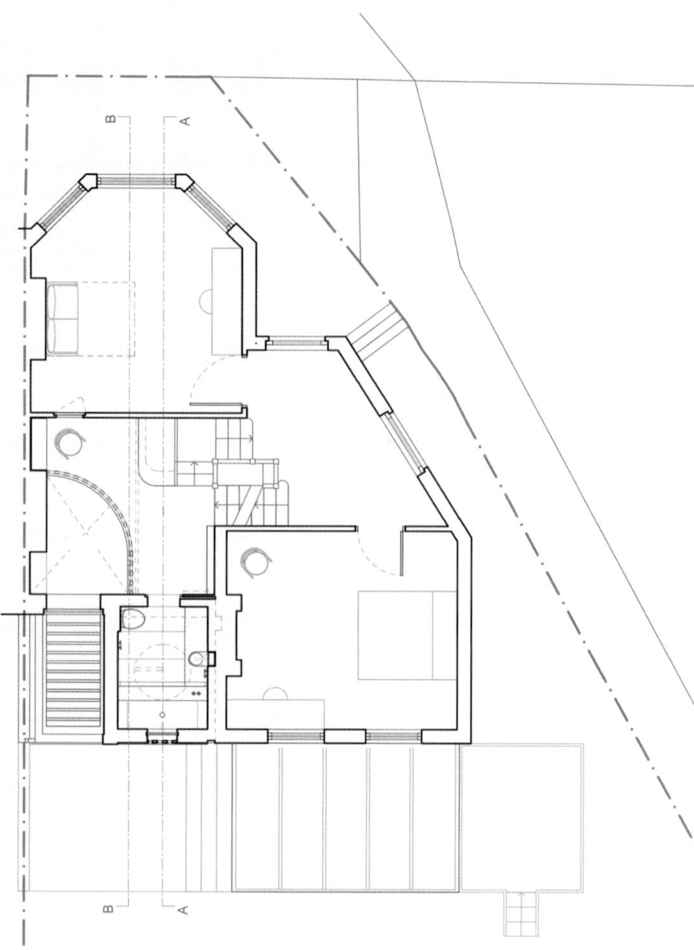

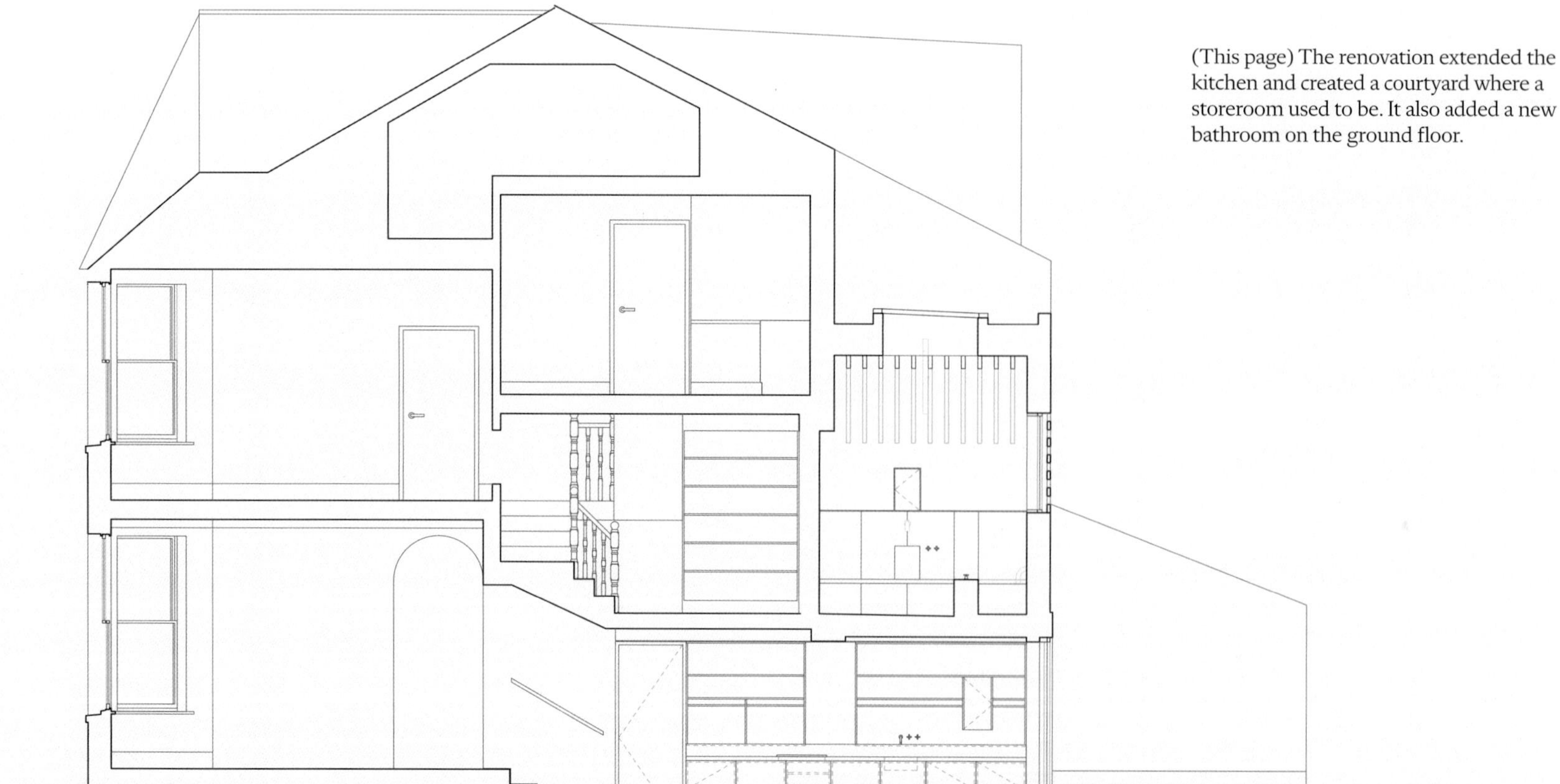

(This page) The renovation extended the kitchen and created a courtyard where a storeroom used to be. It also added a new bathroom on the ground floor.

A Minimalist Modular-Housing Solution

HOMEFUL SYSTEM BY AIXOPLUC ARCHITECTURES
REUS, SPAIN
PHOTOGRAPHY STUDIO → MODULAR HOME PROTOTYPE

Spanish architecture firm Aixopluc created a sustainable modular system to swiftly turn disused buildings into cost-effective housing. Homeful System was developed as an inhabitable prototype and installed in an abandoned photography studio beneath the firm's workshop. Rather than removing existing structures, the system is formed using a series of modular timber constructions made from poplar plywood—grown and manufactured locally—to provide a low-material impact solution to housing demand. The system can be assembled in a DIY fashion on-site, thus reducing the cost of labor. In this prototype, the clean aesthetic of the timberwork complements the uncovered hydraulic-cement tiling and patina of age on the building's white brick walls. The original wooden beams were reinforced, the walls insulated, and terrazzo was used for benches, sinks, and the bathroom. A minimalist's delight, the user can alter the soft-toned timber to make it adaptable for broad-spectrum use.

(Opposite) A tiny timber house in the center of the room acts as a cocoon for a bed. (Above) Each piece is small and light enough to be carried through narrow streets and up stairs.

The architects restored and polished hydraulic-cement tiles that were found under the previous paving. Plywood, cork, and exposed lighting accentuate the building's original features.

From a Printing Factory to a Green Office Abode

MYOUGADANI HOUSE BY MAMM DESIGN
TOKYO, JAPAN
PRINTING FACTORY → RESIDENCE AND OFFICE

In a neighborhood historically known for bookbinding and printing, it's no surprise that this reinforced-concrete building was built as a dual printing factory and residence in the late 1980s. About a decade ago, the second owner transformed the whole building into a residence, and Mamm Design redesigned it once again into the studio's own office and residence. The studio described the remodel of the property as a "rediscovery," as certain parts of the building were stripped back to reveal surprising structural assets. When one staircase was removed to create a light well that spans from the basement to the penthouse, the stairs' metal reinforcements were deemed too beautiful to remove, and were repurposed as a "green staircase" climbing trellis for plants. Now, stripped back to its bones, fountains of plants spill down through the light well, raw concrete remains appealingly rough overhead, and skeletal staircases are unimposing and add a lightweight feel to the home.

(Opposite) Plants abound on the facade of Myougadani House, hinting at what lies within. (Above) A waterfall of greenery tumbles through a former staircase-turned-light well.

Lightweight staircases and a ladder to the roof minimally impose on the home's design, allowing light to flow between levels while imbuing the industrial building with a delicate aesthetic.

Pops of Color Form a Bright and Playful Apartment

NON BOXY LOFTY BY FRAHER & FINDLAY
LONDON, U.K.
APARTMENT → ROOFTOP LOFT EXTENSION

An inner-city apartment in need of modernization, Non Boxy Lofty is a rooftop loft extension by Fraher & Findlay designed to increase the space of a first-floor apartment. Externally, the new loft roof is clad with red zinc rather than traditional slate. The kitchen and dining areas were placed at the top of the extension, looking out over the surrounding rooftops, with the bedrooms below. To ensure copious light in the living spaces, a perforated metal staircase connects the two levels, while a whimsical use of color and geometric touches bring joy to this home. The interior is bright and playful: in the kitchen, a white, apricot, and emerald terrazzo bench is matched with emerald-green cabinetry and pops of apricot on the chairs and dishes. The apricot continues as a feature color in the bedrooms, while the bathroom becomes a geometric playground with pastel pink, green, and white tiles and an unexpected blue sink. Parquetry floors and tastefully curated furniture meet in the living area, where a forest-green velvet couch perches before an olive-green wall.

(Opposite) The natural red-zinc and sedum roof of the loft extension complements the surrounding warm brickwork tones and traditional slate roof tiles, yet its modern aesthetic stands out.

Dark colors accent the home's sharp geometric shapes. Charcoal paint creates the illusion of a triangular railing on the balcony (opposite), while green embellishes the inside slope of the roof (above, left).

LEON

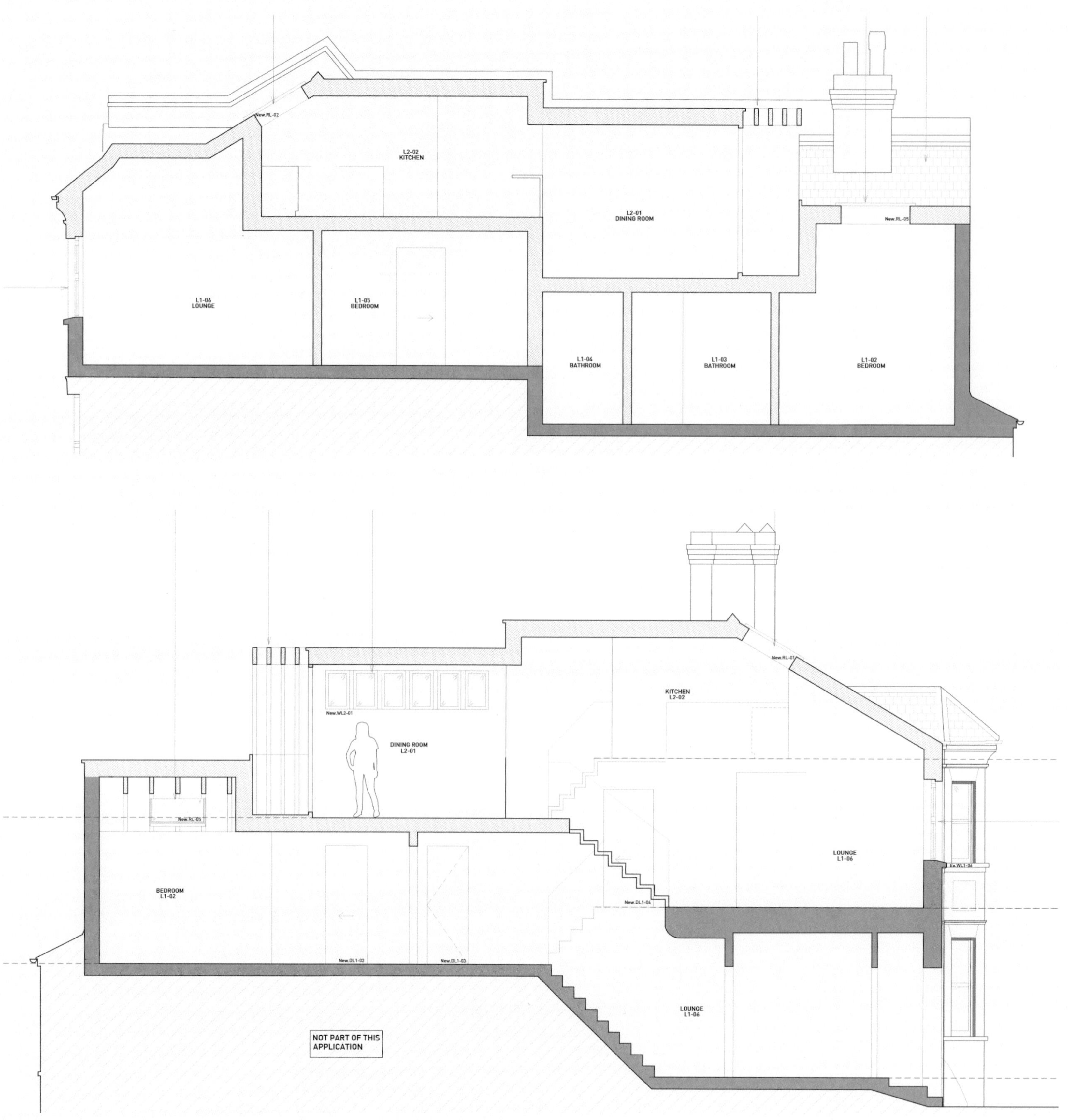

The floor plan of Non Boxy Lofty was extended and redesigned to increase space while prioritizing light. The inverted living plan features communal living spaces above and bedrooms below.

Modern Glass Meets a Historic Mountain Home

THE GLASS CABIN BY MJÖLK ARCHITEKTI
JIZERKA, CZECH REPUBLIC
MOUNTAIN CABIN → GLASS EXTENSION

Toeing the mountainous border between the Czech Republic and Poland, The Glass Cabin also toes the line between contrast and harmony, old and new. Mjölk Architekti extended and renovated this 130-year-old cabin, located in the Jizera Mountains. The cabin remains inconspicuous from its facade, but on the lower floor, the architects removed an annex at the back and extended the living space with a glass mass. For the architects, it was essential not to remove the cabin's "intangible soul," including the fragrance of the timber and the sturdiness of the granite blocks—materials that were both sourced nearby. What has been added acts to complement the traditional home without competing with the past. The glass extension hosts a slightly sunken living room with a shiny, brass-clad ceiling and a white-tiled fireplace. Elements of the extension are brought through into the original structure; for example, there is now a glass floor where parts of the original timber floor could not be salvaged.

(Above) Large glass windows, a shimmering brass-clad ceiling, and a warming fireplace combine to create a magical relaxation zone with expansive views of the surrounding idyllic countryside.

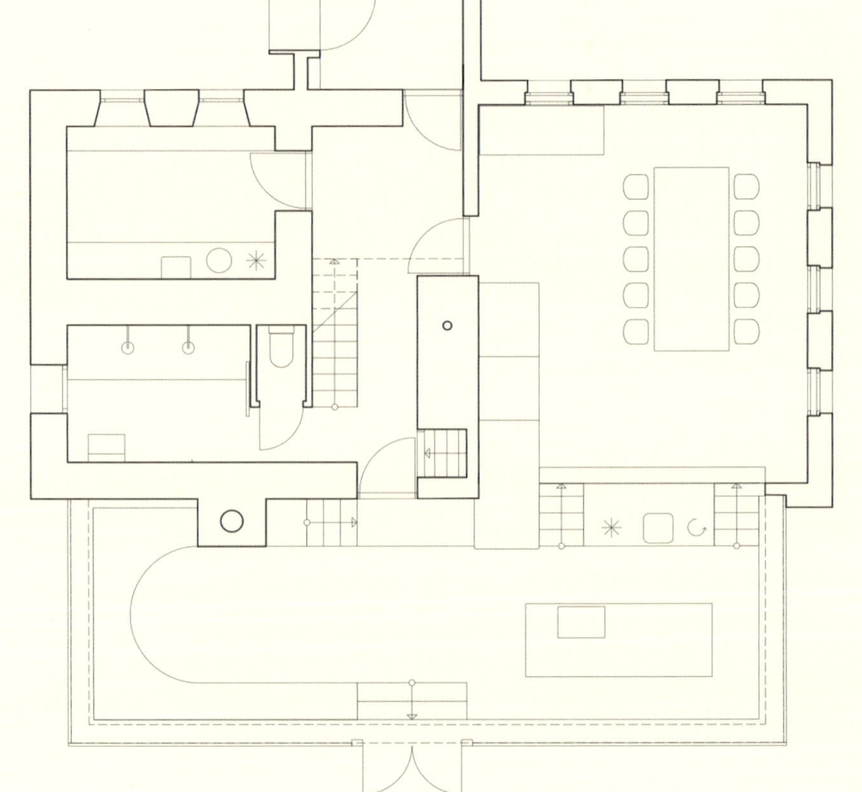

(Above and opposite) The kitchen and dining room retain a humble energy true to the original form of the house, with cozy timber floors, walls, and a low ceiling.

(Opposite) The upper floor is accessed via steel stairs. Rotten or deteriorated timber floors were replaced with glass, providing unexpected views through the home.

A Traditional Gabled Home with a Modern Touch

HOUSE VDG BY GRAUX & BAEYENS ARCHITECTEN
KOKSIJDE, BELGIUM
VACATION HOME → PERMANENT RESIDENCE

A decidedly traditional exterior gives way to a refreshed, contemporary interior in this typical Belgian *fermette,* or farmhouse, redesigned to increase space, light, and update the floor plan. To accommodate these changes, a second gabled roof volume that mimics the archetypal seaside house design was inserted at a 90-degree angle to the original. The new wing holds a dining area that overlooks the garden and features a triangular window at the tip of the gabled ceiling, illuminating the loftiness of the room. At the intersection of the original and the new volumes, a sleek white spiral staircase leads to the bathroom and five bedrooms, allowing enough space for the family to share. The outdated 1970s interior was refurbished with contemporary details, such as a concrete bench cast alongside the kitchen that provides an outdoor seating area from which to enjoy the sunlight. Once the renovation was complete, the owner decided to make the former weekend home her permanent residence.

A new volume sits perpendicular to, and within, the existing house. Its roof tiles and gabled design merge with the original, but larger windows and speckled masonry reveals its modernity.

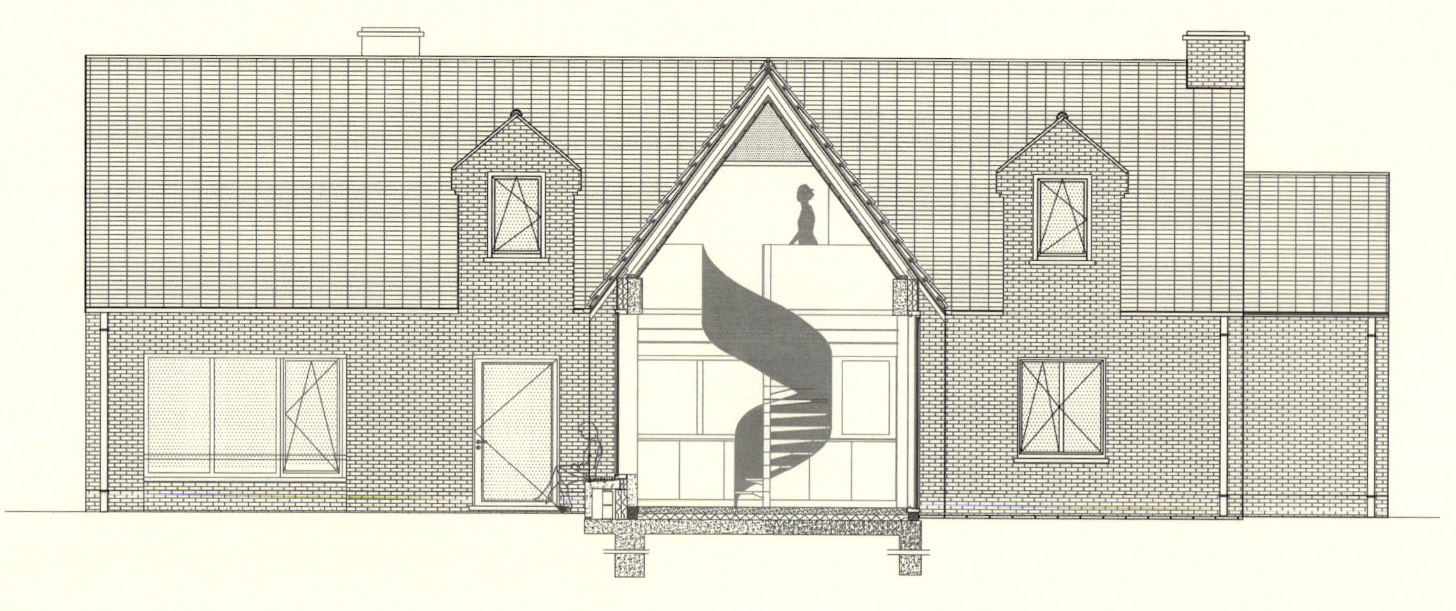

(Above and opposite) The spiral staircase marks the intersection of the old and the new wings of the home, separating the kitchen and loft from the dining area in the new wing.

(Above) Pierre Jeanneret's Easy chairs sit on a colorful rug in front of a subtle black fireplace in the living room. Holes in the wall offer sight lines between the communal areas.

A Dilapidated Farmer's Cottage Modernized

NIEBY CROFTERS COTTAGE BY JAN HENRIK JANSEN AND STUDIO MARSHALL BLECHER
NIEBY, GERMANY
TENANT FARMER'S COTTAGE → MODERN RESIDENCE

Surrounded by barley fields and facing the marshy Geltinger Birk nature reserve is Nieby Crofters Cottage. Abandoned for over a decade, the home was dilapidated and the roof had partially collapsed. The home had low ceilings and a pig sty, and sheds had been tacked to its rear. The architects sought to modernize the home yet stay true to its historic style—a vernacular that is slowly disappearing from the area. The streetside facade was maintained, but at the back, the home's peaked thatched roof charmingly contrasts with substantial modern alterations. Large black-framed windows are cut into the historic brick, partitioning a sunken outdoor terrace from the interior, oak-lined living space. The center of the home—once a maze of 14 rooms—is now a spacious kitchen and dining room, with a chapel-like ceiling. German oak joinery, doors, and furniture feature throughout, while sustainability considerations ensure a high level of insulation with under-floor heating and triple-glazed windows.

(Left) Architects Jan Henrik Jansen and Marshall Blecher contrasted the historic craftsmanship of an original thatched roof with a bold and elegant new glass extension.

(Opposite) In the kitchen, an impressive concrete island—which was craned in while the roof was being repaired—acts as both a kitchen countertop and a dining table, surrounded by Wishbone chairs.

A Farmhouse Ruin Repurposed as a Retreat

SCHEDLBERG BY PETER HAIMERL
ARNBRUCK, GERMANY
FARMHOUSE → RETREAT AND SEMINAR SPACE

One of very few existing historic Bavarian farmhouses, this log-and-granite cabin was abandoned in 1963, slowly becoming "more soil than architecture," according to architect Peter Haimerl. Grazing livestock began to use it for shelter, and nature slowly overtook the abode with time. When Haimerl began the project, the outer wall was still intact, holding the ridge purlin, but the structure was unfortunately close to collapse. Mossy granite bars sourced from near the front door were converted into concrete bars and used as support for the decaying wood. These beams create a sense of pixelation when viewing the home from a distance, reflecting the undulation of the original stonework on a grander scale. Where possible, the original timber, stone masonry, and windows and doors remain, supplemented with cement, glass, and a muted palette of grays and cool timbers in keeping with the building's origin. The farmhouse has been repurposed into what Haimerl calls "contemplative architecture," as it is now used for seminars and retreats.

(Opposite) Staggered concrete bars renew and infuse a contemporary aesthetic into a section of the home that was beyond repair. (Above) The original windows were kept when possible.

(Above) Original doors with weathered patinas were kept whenever possible. A small nook in the living area was transformed into a cozy table for dining or working.

18
16

The Fresh Face of a Farmer's Mountain Shelter

LÙ CHATARME BY DESCHENAUX FOLLONIER
AROLLA, SWITZERLAND
MOUNTAIN SHELTER → MINIMALIST CHALET

Located near the village of Arolla at the far end of the Val d'Hérens, this mountain shelter sits at 6,070 feet (1,850 meters) above sea level. Each year, the owner climbs to the mountain chalet to let his cows graze while living there for a few months. The farmer wanted some features to remain while also enhancing its hosting potential and comfort. The original main wooden room was preserved with the addition of a subtle timber staircase leading upstairs. The first floor was updated to sleep six people and renovated using timber from a nearby larch forest owned by the farmer's family. A concrete extension—which the architects refer to as the "mineral" part of the chalet—sits between the original construction and the rock face beside it, roughly following the natural curvature of the landscape. Here, the iron-oxide color of the rock is mimicked in the tone of the timber window frames. The project was executed with care and effort due to the altitude and a river barrier, meaning that much of the work had to be done by hand.

The modern concrete extension to Lù Chatarme gently abuts a mountainous stone wall, coming just inches from touching it. The construction does not seek to alter the surrounding nature.

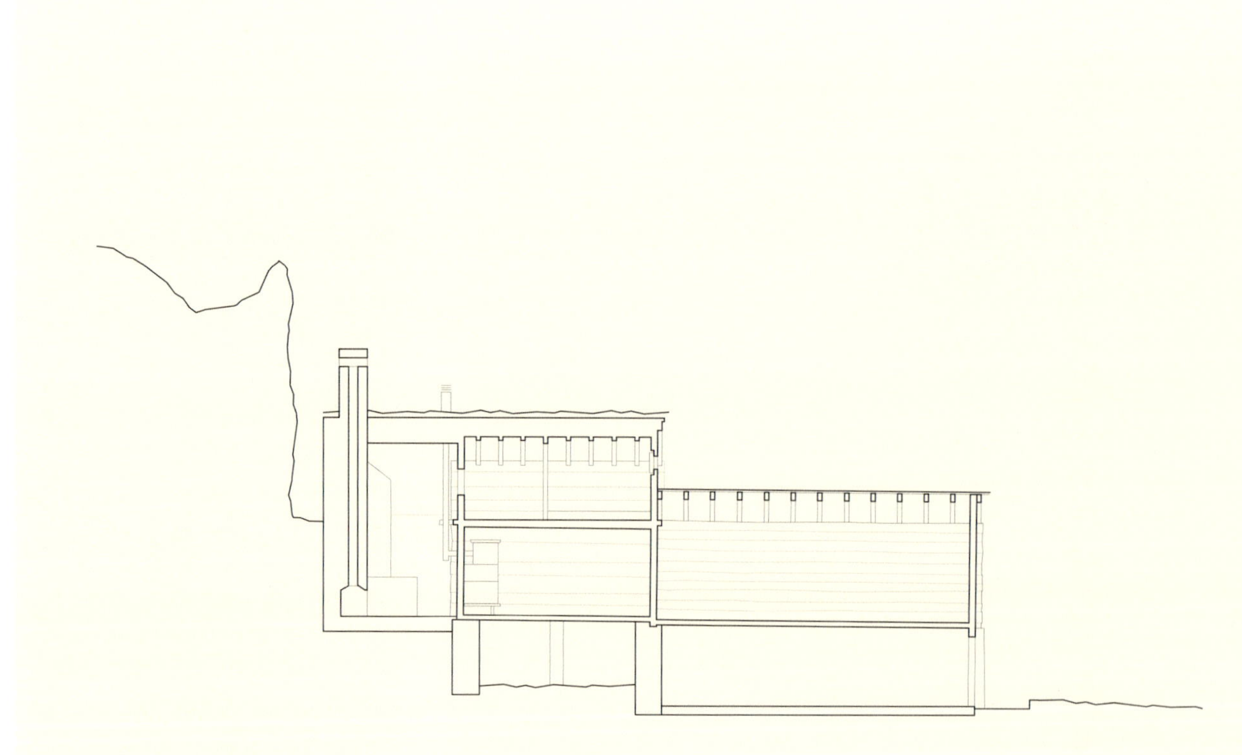

Raw concrete sits alongside timber, giving the home a natural vibe. The concrete is side by side with the exterior stone, mirroring the minerality of the local landscape.

A Stone Masonry Barn Becomes a Compact Home

BORNET HOUSE BY SAVIOZ FABRIZZI ARCHITECTES
OLLON, SWITZERLAND
DILAPIDATED BARN → MODERN HOME

Through a process of care and patience, Bornet House was built from a former dilapidated barn. The lower level once housed livestock, while the upper floor formerly stocked hay. Constructed using the original structure of undulating stone-rubble masonry, making the house liveable was a delicate process due to the proximity of other houses and the instability of the walls. The lower level's shaky stone walls were cautiously extended, and the ground was partially excavated to have enough height in both floors and to insulate the ground floor. The west wall, which needed to be reconstructed, now has a large window spanning its width that provides wide views across the valley. Other existing openings were retained in the same places. Inside, black-stained wooden board covers the walls and the pitched ceiling, and underfoot, the exposed concrete-slab flooring is also stained black to match. The repurposing of this barn means that this modern home follows the vernacular of the location while sustainably reusing materials.

Due to its slope-side positioning, the home had unobstructed space on one side. Taking advantage of this, the architects devised a large living room window overlooking the Rhône Valley.

(Above) The rubble masonry moves downhill with the natural gradient of the land. The design retained existing openings on the ground floor, with wooden screens installed above.

Ruins Inspire the Redesign of a French Farmhouse

HOURRÉ BY COLLECTIF ENCORE
LABASTIDE-VILLEFRANCHE, FRANCE
BASQUE FARMHOUSE RUIN → FAMILY HOME

Fiercely connected to the outdoors, Collectif Encore transformed Hourré from a dilapidated farmhouse to a family home designed to encourage social connection and a life incorporated with nature. The architects integrated two large nets as spaces for relaxation and activities—at times resembling a playground. One of the vast hammock-like nets hangs beside a trail of vines on the exterior of the white and green home. The interior echoes a collapse that happened when the building was unused: the ceiling had fallen through the upper-level floor, creating a large clearing above the main room. Here, another net hovers above the living area, connecting the two levels. The home merges with its surroundings, capitalizing on its optimal climate. On the ground floor, greenery overtakes one corner of a covered terrace and spacious openings connect the interior to the outdoors. The upper-level bathroom roof gives way to a vast aperture, revealing the sky and views at the border of the Béarn region and the Basque region of France.

(Left) The house was left as open as possible, allowing it to intimately connect with nature. This large covered balcony is a space for eating, playing, and relaxing.

(Opposite) Sliding doors are mounted on exterior facades so that they disappear when open; furniture is kept simple, allowing the space to feel uncluttered.

(Right) The exposed bathroom catches sun during the day. Surrounded by three walls, it manages to retain heat relatively well.

15 LOVE SONGS
FOR
JULIEN & ANNA

Calm Interiors in Iceland's Wild Outdoors

HLÖÐUBERG STUDIO BY STUDIO BUA
SKARÐSSTRÖND, ICELAND
REMOTE BARN → RESIDENCE AND ART STUDIO

A dilapidated concrete barn with a corrugated steel roof in rural western Iceland was transformed into a two-level family home and art studio. Much of the barn's unique character was preserved; lichen growth on the outer walls was retained and pebble aggregate merges the structure with the earth. A ruined lean-to addition remains as a sheltered courtyard, and crumbling perimeter walls were left untouched to enclose a new flower and vegetable garden. Echoing the original roof, a gabled second level was built from a timber structure clad in corrugated aluzinc—one of the few materials able to withstand the site's harsh environment and extreme weather—and slotted into the original walls. The interior hosts a robust ground floor with a kitchen, dining room, and a double-height art studio, while upstairs are bedrooms and a living room. The calm materiality means it doesn't detract from displayed art, and the surrounding meadow's seasonal colors inspired the palette. A ground-source heat pump provides sufficient and sustainable under-floor heating, paired with triple-glazed windows.

The windows in the new upper level allow extensive views across meadows, mountains, and Breiðafjörður, a large shallow bay in western Iceland.

(This page) The structure needed to act as both a home and a working artist's studio. Studio Bua replaced a large corrugated-steel roof while aiming to preserve much of the original character.

An Antique Barn Becomes an Intimate Chalet

CONVERSION IN CENTRAL VALAIS BY SAVIOZ FABRIZZI ARCHITECTES
VALAIS, SWITZERLAND
PASTURE BARN → MINIMALIST CHALET

Set in the mountainous green slopes of central Valais, Switzerland, this alpine pasture chalet, or *mayen,* was converted from an early 20th-century barn. The architects retained the original barn's format, utilizing the natural gradient of the land; on the lower level, a masonry base provides support for the upper timber layer. The upper section strikes a balance between openness and privacy by integrating with the stunning natural surroundings while providing cozy places to relax. Giving direct access to the exterior and allowing airflow across the house, floor-to-ceiling glass that can be fully opened flanks the double-height central kitchen and dining room. Contrastingly, the living room and the mezzanine—which was converted into an additional bedroom—are encapsulated with timber, creating a refuge of warmth and peace. On the lower level, the main bedroom and bathroom are the most private and intimate parts of the minimalist chalet.

(This page) From the open kitchen, a simple ladder leads up to a mezzanine bedroom. (Opposite) The chalet sits on a slope in one of Switzerland's sparsely populated alpine regions.

(Right) The home is perforated, which separates the timber and masonry sections. This reinforces the transverse effect and minimizes the need for other openings in the outer walls.

A

ACHA ZABALLA ARCHITECTS
achazaballa.com

Loft Study House #1
Bilbao, Spain
Year of the original project: 2005
Year of renovation: 2021
Photography: Luis Díaz Díaz
luisdiazdiaz.com
pp. 32–35

AIXOPLUC ARCHITECTURES
aixopluc.net

Homeful System
Reus, Spain
Year of the original project: 1919
Year of renovation: 2019
Photography: José Hevia
josehevia.es
pp. 192–195

ANGELUCCI ARCHITECTS
angelucciarchitects.com

Il Nido House
Melbourne, Australia
Year of the original project: 1885
Year of renovation: 2021
Builder: Belarte Building Group
Furniture & styling: Fenton & Fenton
Photography: Dylan James
dylanjames.com.au
pp. 22, 23 bottom, 25 bottom, 27 bottom left
Dave Kulesza
davekulesza.com
pp. 23 top, 24, 25 top, 26 top and bottom right, 42, 184 bottom
Gerrit Rietveld, Cassina Chair
© VG Bild-Kunst, Bonn 2023
pp. 23, 25

ARCHMONGERS ARCHITECTS
archmongers.com

Little Brownings
London, U.K.
Year of the original project: 1960s
Year of renovation: 2019
Photography: French + Tye
frenchandtye.com
pp. 28–31

AUBA STUDIO
aubastudio.com

NZ10 Renovation
Palma, Spain
Year of the original project: 1953, renovated in 1980
Year of renovation: 2020
Stools: Studio Jaia
Structure: Hima estructuras
Photography: José Hevia
josehevia.es
pp. 86–89

AUX
Bureau voor architectuur en stedenbouw
aux.be

Brewery Conversion
Ghent, Belgium
Year of the original project: c. 1900
Year of renovation: 2018
Photography: Luc Roymans
roymans.com
pp. 40, 70–75, 143

B

BENTHEM CROUWEL ARCHITECTS
benthemcrouwel.com

Vijzelgracht House
Amsterdam, Netherlands
Year of the original project: 1670
Year of renovation: 2021
Photography: Jannes Linders
janneslinders.nl
pp. 114–119, 145

BLAF ARCHITECTEN
blaf.be

tmSN House
Sint-Niklaas, Belgium
Year of the original project: 19th century
Year of renovation: 2017
Photography: Stijn Bollaert
stijnbollaert.com
pp. 124–127

BURR STUDIO
burr.studio

MG08
Madrid, Spain
Year of the original project: 1950
Year of renovation: 2020
Builders: Proingenia proyectos
Kitchen: Burr + Cubro Design
Photography: José Hevia
josehevia.es
pp. 12–17

C

CHAOFFICE
chaoffice.info

House over the Wall
Beijing, China
Year of the original project: 19th century, alterations c. 1940 and 1970
Year of renovation: 2022
Photography: Cheng Zhi
pp. 176–181

COLLECTIF ENCORE
Anna and Julien Chavepayre
collectifencore.com

Hourré
Labastide-Villefranche, France
Year of the original project: c. 1700
Year of renovation: 2015
Photography: Michel Bonvin
michelbonvin.ch
pp. 43, 238–245

MARIE COMBETTE AND DANIEL MORENO FLORES/ LA CABINA DE LA CURIOSIDAD
lacabinadelacuriosidad.com

Cholan Nests House
Perucho, Ecuador
Year of the original project: unknown
Year of renovation: 2022
Architecture team: David Rodríguez
Engineer: Patricio Cevallos
Construction: Luis Guamán, Daniel Cepeda, Paul Cepeda, Luis Araque, and Italo Vita
Illustrations: Carlos Valverde
Photography: Jag Studio
jagstudio.ec
pp. 48–51

D

MARIE-ANNE DERVILLE
marieannederville.com

Hôtel d'Hallwyl
Paris, France
Year of the original project: mid 18th century
Year of renovation: 1998
Photography: Matthew Avignone, courtesy of Marie-Anne Derville
p. 142
Andrée Putman, Clawfoot Tub
© VG Bild-Kunst, Bonn 2023
p. 142

DESCHENAUX FOLLONIER
valentindeschenaux.ch

Lù Chatarme
Arolla, Switzerland
Year of the original project: c. 1860
Year of renovation: 2019
Photography: Joël Tettamanti
tettamanti.ch
pp. 230–233

DMVA ARCHITECTS
dmva-architecten.be

House TP
Mechelen, Belgium
Year of the original project: 1850
Year of renovation: 2017
Photography: Bart Gosselin
bartgosselin.com
pp. 18–21

F

FEINA STUDIO
feinastudio.com

Plywood House
Palma de Mallorca, Spain
Year of the original project: 1920s
Years of renovation: 2016
Photography: Luis Díaz Díaz
luisdiazdiaz.com
p. 4

JOSEP FERRANDO ARCHITECTURE
josepferrando.com

House E+M
Sant Cugat del Vallès, Spain
Year of the original project: early 20th century
Year of renovation: 2014
Photography: Adrià Goula
adriagoula.com
pp. 80–85

FRAHER & FINDLAY
fraherandfindlay.com

Non Boxy Lofty
London, U.K.
Year of the original project: 1905
Year of renovation: 2021
Interior design: client
Photography: Chris Wharton
chriswharton.photography
pp. 202–209

G

过半儿 GUÒ BÀN ÉR

The Roof House
Beijing, China
Year of the original project: 1980
Year of renovation: 2022
Photography: Boris Shiu
borisshiuphoto.com
pp. 112 left, 134–139

GRAUX & BAEYENS ARCHITECTEN
graux-baeyens.be

House C-VL
De Haan, Belgium
Year of the original project: 1960
Year of renovation: 2017
Photography: Jeroen Verrecht
jeroenverrecht.com
pp. 128–133

House VDG
Koksijde, Belgium
Year of the original project: 1970
Years of renovation: 2017–2021
Photography: Stijn Bollaert
stijnbollaert.com
pp. 78 top, 216–221
Pierre Jeanneret, Easy Chairs
© VG Bild-Kunst, Bonn 2023
p. 221

H

PETER HAIMERL
peterhaimerl.com

Schedlberg
Arnbruck, Germany
Year of the original project: late 18th century
Year of renovation: 2017
Photography: Edward Beierle
beierlegoerlich.com
pp. 226–229

HÉ! ARCHITECTUUR
he-architectuur.be

Karper
Brussels, Belgium
Year of the original project: 19th century
Year of renovation: 2023
Photography: Tim Van de Velde
tvdv.be
pp. 110, 144, 152–159

J

JAN HENRIK JANSEN AND STUDIO MARSHALL BLECHER
janhenrikjansen.dk
marshallblecher.com

Nieby Crofters Cottage
Nieby, Germany
Year of the original project: late 19th century
Year of renovation: 2022
Photography: José Campos
josecamposphotographer.com
pp. 222–225

K

KESSLER PLESCHER ARCHITEKTEN
kesslerplescher.de

Dr. Funk
Buggenhagen, Germany
Year of the original project: 1960s
Year of renovation: 2022
Photography: Schnepp Renou
schnepp-renou.com
pp. 112 right, 120–123

M

MAMM DESIGN
mamm-design.com

Myougadani House
Tokyo, Japan
Year of the original project: 1987
Year of renovation: 2020
Structural engineer: Shuji Tada
Structural design /
Lighting design: Toh Design
Photography: Takumi Ota
pp. 78 bottom, 196–201

MJÖLK ARCHITEKTI
mjolk.cz

The Glass Cabin
Jizerka, Czech Republic
Year of the original project: 1890
Year of renovation: 2020
Windows: Janošík
Furniture: Sollus
Tiled stoves: Dtile
Photography: BoysPlayNice
boysplaynice.com
pp. 210–215

O

YUTAROU OHTA
yutrohta.studio.site

K/door House
Gunma Prefecture, Japan
Year of the original project: 1962
Year of renovation: 2022
Photography: Takashi Uemura
takashiuemura.com
pp. 102–105

P

PLAN COMÚN
plancomun.com

La Fage
Saint-Beauzile, France
Year of the original project: 16th century
Year of renovation: 2019
Main structure: S.N.R.B
Plumbing: Jean Béhar
Electricity: Bailliet
Photography: Maxime Verret
maximeverret.com
pp. 44–51

POINT SUPREME ARCHITECTS
pointsupreme.com

Ilioupoli Apartment
Athens, Greece
Year of the original project: mid 20th century
Year of renovation: 2020
Photography: Yiannis Hadjaslanis
hadjiaslanis.com
pp. 66–69, 142 top

R

VLADIMIR RADUTNY ARCHITECTS
radutny.com

Michigan Loft
Chicago, IL, USA
Year of the original project: early 1900s
Year of renovation: 2017–2018
Photography: Mike Schwartz Photography
mikeschwartzphoto.com
pp. 56–59

S

RAÚL SÁNCHEZ ARCHITECTS
raulsanchezarchitects.com

BSP 20 House
Barcelona, Spain
Year of the original project:
late 19th century
Years of renovation: 2013–2022
Photography: José Hevia
josehevia.es
pp. 6–11

SAVIOZ FABRIZZI ARCHITECTES
sf-ar.ch

Bornet House
Ollon, Switzerland
Year of the original project: c. 1800
Year of renovation: 2017
Photography: Thomas Jantscher
jantscher.ch
pp. 234–237

Conversion in Central Valais
Valais, Switzerland
Year of the original project: c. 1900
Year of renovation: 2017
Photography: Thomas Jantscher
jantscher.ch
pp. 250–253

SERBOLI BUREAU AND COLOMBO ARCHITECTURE
serbolibureau.com
colomboarchitecture.com

Palau Apartment
Barcelona, Spain
Year of the original project: c. 1800
Year of renovation: 2022
Photography: Roberto Ruiz
robertoruiz.eu
p. 79

Rocha Apartment
Barcelona, Spain
Year of the original project:
early 20th century
Year of renovation: 2014
Photography: Roberto Ruiz
robertoruiz.eu
pp. 146–151

SÍOL STUDIOS
siolstudios.com

18th Street Loft
San Francisco, CA, USA
Year of the original project: 1920
Year of renovation: 2020
Photography: Joe Fletcher
joefletcher.com
pp. 52–55, 113

SO&CO.
so-co.org

Residential Extension in Kanamachi
Tokyo, Japan
Year of the original project: 2001
Year of renovation: 2020
Structural design: Enhanced
Quality Structure Design
Construction company: Daisaku
Photography: Hayato Wakabayashi
wakabayashihayato.com
pp. 98–101

SPACE ENCOUNTERS
space-encounters.eu

BD House
Bergen, Netherlands
Year of the original project: 1950s
Year of renovation: 2022
Photography: Lorenzo Zandri
lorenzozandri.com
pp. 170–175

STUDIO ANDREW TROTTER, GAVALAS IOANNIDOU ARCHITECTURE, AND EVA PAPADAKI
andrew-trotter.com
gavalasioannidou.com

10AM Lofts
Athens, Greece
Year of the original project: 1970s
Year of renovation: unknown
Photography: Salva Lopez
salvalopez.com
pp. 160–165
Charlotte Perriand, Dordogne Chair
©VG Bild-Kunst, Bonn 2023
p. 161

STUDIO BEN ALLEN
studiobenallen.com

The House Recast
London, U.K.
Year of the original project: 19th century
Year of renovation: 2021
Structural engineer: Entuitive
Landscape design: Daniel Bell Landskap
Contractor: Peridot
Structural and exterior concrete:
Cornish Concrete Products
Interior concrete: Concreations
Photography: French + Tye
frenchandtye.com
pp. 140, 186–191

STUDIO BUA
studiobua.com

Hlöðuberg Studio
Skarðsströnd, Iceland
Year of the original project: 1937
Year of renovation: 2021
Contractor: Eiríkur Kristjánsson
Structural engineer: Gísli Guðmundsson
Photography: Marino Thorlacius
marinothorlacius.com
pp. 246–249

STUDIO OKAMI
studiookami.com

RST 13/14
Antwerp, Belgium
Year of the original project: 1972
Year of renovation: 2021
Photography: Tim Van de Velde
tvdv.be
pp. 60–65, 76

STUDIO WEAVE
studioweave.com

Made of Sand
Axminster, U.K.
Year of the original project: c. 1700
Year of renovation: 2019
Engineering: Momentum
Photography: Jim Stephenson
clickclickjim.com
pp. 166–169

T

YOSHICHIKA TAKAGI + ASSOCIATES
yoshichikatakagi.com

The Row House of Western Sunlight
Sapporo, Japan
Year of the original project: 1975
Year of renovation: 2021
Photography: Ikuya Sasaki
ikuyasasaki.com
pp. 94–97

The Deformed Roof House of Furano
Furano, Japan
Year of the original project: 1974
Year of renovation: 2018
Photography: Ikuya Sasaki
ikuyasasaki.com
pp. 106–109

TD-ATELIER
td-ms.com

House in Shimogamo
Kyoto, Japan
Year of the original project: 1980
Year of renovation: 2020
Landscape architecture:
Michikusa / Ogasahara Satoru
Photography: Kohei Matsumura
matsumurakohei.com
pp. 90–93

V

VALLRIBERA ARQUITECTES
vallriberaarquitectes.com

105JON
Vallès Occidental, Spain
Year of the original project: 1925
Year of renovation: 2020
Photography: José Hevia
josehevia.es
pp. 36–39

Upgrade Your House

Rebuild, Renovate, and Reimagine Your Home

This book was conceived, edited, and designed by *gestalten.*

Edited by *Robert Klanten* and *Masha Erman*

Editorial support by *Effie Efthymiadi*

Introduction and features by *Lilly Jean Cao*

Project texts and captions by *Laura Box*

Editorial Management: *Arndt Jasper*

Photo Editor: *Zoe Paterniani*

Design, layout, and cover by *Melanie Ullrich*

Typeface: Flecha by *Rui Abreu*

Cover image: Dr. Funk by *Kessler Plescher Architekten* / photo: *Schnepp Renou*

Backcover image: NZ10 Renovation by *Auba Studio* / photo: *José Hevia*

Printed by Tuijtel, Netherlands
Made in Europe

Published by gestalten, Berlin 2023
ISBN 978-3-96704-112-5

For more information, and to order books, please visit www.gestalten.com

Bibliographic information published by the Deutsche Nationalbibliothek. The Deutsche Nationalbibliothek lists this publication in the Deutsche Nationalbibliografie; detailed bibliographic data is available online at www.dnb.de

None of the content in this book was published in exchange for payment by commercial parties or designers; the inclusion of all work is based solely on its artistic merit.

This book was printed on paper certified according to the standards of the FSC®.